PSYCHOTHERAPY AND THE MODIFICATION
OF ABNORMAL BEHAVIOR

McGraw-Hill Paperback Series in Psychopathology

Norman Garmezy, *Consulting Editor*

Holzman: Psychoanalysis and Psychopathology

Maher: Introduction to Research in Psychopathology

Strupp: Psychotherapy and the Modification of Abnormal Behavior: An Introduction to Theory and Research

Forthcoming Books in Series:

Basowitz: Psychosomatic Disorders: Research and Theory

Becker: Manic-depressive Disorders: Research and Theory

Cohen: Biological Research and Theory in Psychopathology

Dahlstrom: Assessment of Psychopathological Behavior

Garmezy: Schizophrenia: Research and Theory

Goodrich: Disorders of Childhood: Research and Theory

Kalish and Geer: Learning Theory and Psychopathology

Parsons: Organic Disorders: Research and Theory

Rosenthal: Genetics of Psychopathology

Solomon, Kramer, and Wechsler: Social Psychological Approaches to Psychopathology: Research and Theory

Speisman: Neurotic Disorders: Research and Theory

West: Experimental Induction of Psychopathological States

Hans H. Strupp

Professor of Psychology
Vanderbilt University

Psychotherapy and the Modification of Abnormal Behavior:

An Introduction to Theory and Research

McGraw-Hill Book Company

New York   St. Louis   San Francisco   Düsseldorf
Johannesburg   Kuala Lumpur   London   Mexico   Montreal   New Delhi
Panama   Rio de Janeiro   Singapore   Sydney   Toronto

To the memory of my parents,

Josef and Anna Strupp

PSYCHOTHERAPY AND THE
MODIFICATION OF ABNORMAL BEHAVIOR:
An Introduction to Theory and Research

Library of Congress Catalog Card Number 78-128793

ISBN 07-062230-2
    07-062231-0
3 4 5 6 7 8 9 0 VBVB 7 9 8 7 6 5 4 3 2 1

This book was set in Caledonia by Vail-Ballou Press, Inc., and printed on permanent paper and bound by Vail-Ballou Press, Inc. The cover was designed by Edward A. Butler; the drawings were done by John Cordes, J. & R. Technical Services, Inc. The editors were Walter Maytham and Paula Henson. Peter D. Guilmette supervised production.

Editor's Introduction

This is an optimistic and reasoned book about a process (and a profession) that has known more than its share of slings and arrows. How else can one describe the rueful definition suggested by one academician that psychotherapy was "an unidentified technique applied to unspecified problems with unpredictable outcomes." Shorn of its irony, what this critic was suggesting some two decades ago was that the efficacy of psychotherapy was debatable, the diversity of its methods considerable, the assumption of successful outcome worthy of challenge and that the type of patient who could benefit from therapeutic intervention was essentially unknown. Indeed warnings have issued forth from seasoned investigators suggesting that therapy could cause some patients to worsen. Professor Jerome Frank of the Johns Hopkins University is a distinguished investigator of psychotherapy and one fundamentally friendly to the enterprise. Yet he too felt constrained to set forth this warning for his colleagues:

> To be able to show that psychotherapy could do good, researchers first had to find the courage to face the fact that it could also do harm, that psychotherapy made some patients worse has been staring investigators in the face for a long time . . . but they have glossed this over for understandable reasons. It has been customary to report results of psychotherapy in terms of whether patients were improved or unimproved, implying that they could not possibly have been harmed by treatment. In retrospect, it is a strange assumption that psychotherapy could make people better but could not hurt them. Any other remedy that is powerful enough to do good, from aspirin to penicillin, will do harm if misused. There is no reason to think that psychotherapy would be an exception.

This question of just who will benefit from therapy and who will be disadvantaged by it has proved to be an extraordinarily complicated one. Consider for a moment merely a few of the variables that appear to be of significance in this gain-loss problem. First, there is the therapist with his wide-ranging set of personal qualities including the adequacy or inadequacy of his training and his sophistication in understanding the patient (or "client" for the Rogerians and "subject" for the behavioristically minded) and his messages. Second, there is the patient with his own complex personality structure, life history and form of ongoing distress. Third, there is the set of both therapist and patient. For the therapist there is the internalized query: "Can I help this person?" Or more neutrally, perhaps, "Can this person profit from treatment?" For the patient there is an expectancy of hope or despair. Hope is a great healing attribute and patients differ markedly in their belief that here at last is a figure capable of assisting in the resolution of their distress. Yet positive belief—the vaunted placebo effect of medicine—is a powerful factor in all therapies. There are also the learning qualities that characterize therapeutic exchange—the therapist as a model for the patient who searches for more appropriate modes of coping, the pattern of reinforcement contingencies that he provides, the history of the patient that may determine the specific reinforcers that are effective modifiers of his behavior. And, finally, there are the personal qualities of the patient. It was Schofield who coined the term *YAVIS Syndrome* to denote that combination of patient attributes which so many therapists cathect (since it increases the likelihood of favorable outcome): Youthfulness, Attractiveness, Verbal skill, Intelligence, and Successful life style.

Given this complexity, is it any wonder that the appearance in 1952 of Eysenck's landmark review on the results of psychotherapy (which he elaborated upon in 1961 and 1965) evoked a most spirited controversy? Eysenck projected an intensely dismal image of therapeutic outcome in psychotherapy:

> With the single exception of the psychotherapeutic methods based on learning theory, results of published research with military and civilian neurotics, and with both adults and children, suggest that the therapeutic effects of psychotherapy are small or non-existent, and do not in any demonstrable way add to the non-specific effects of routine medical treatment, or to such events as occur in the patients' everyday experience.

Strupp has in the past (and once again in this volume) challenged Eysenck's conclusions with the observation that "it is futile to make judgments and predictions about outcome so long as we have paid insufficient attention to variables in the patient, the therapist, the method of therapy, the patient-therapist interaction, and the surrounding life situation."

What Strupp has suggested is that Eysenck has underestimated the complexity of the very process he has found so wanting. My colleague, Paul Meehl, tends to agree with Eysenck that the present state of scientific evidence places in dispute the efficacious qualities of therapy, but he too enters a significant demurrer. Two factors that influence outcome data trouble Meehl: there are too many patients who simply cannot be helped by therapy, any therapy; and there are too many incompetent therapists incapable of helping even those who can benefit from treatment. Setting forth rather conservative estimates of the number of patients capable of benefiting and the number of therapists capable of assisting, Meehl has suggested that the expectancy for significant favorable results in outcome studies is a marginal one:

> Let us suppose that ¼ represents an upper bound on the proportion of patients currently receiving conventional therapy who are appropriate; and let ¼ also represent an upper bound on the proportion of therapists who are much good at their job. Assuming an essentially random model of patient-therapist pairing, the joint probability of a suitable patient getting to a suitable therapist is around .06 (.25 × .25), a very small tail to wag the statistical dog in outcome studies.

The situation is indeed complicated and these intricate characteristics of psychotherapy (and of research into the process) provide the focus of Professor Strupp's text. He describes the theoretical diversity that exists and the many forms of treatment that have emerged out of these multiple schemas. A significant portion of the volume is given over to research on intervention and its consequences. Strupp has attempted to describe and to discuss questions that now occupy the time and energies of numerous investigators. What makes for patient change? Can it be measured? To what can such changes be attributed? What are the contributions of therapist, patient, and situation to such behavior change?

In discussing these questions, Professor Strupp has chosen a path of optimism rather than despair. His volume bears a distinctive message. It is necessary, he asserts, that for the field of psychotherapy to progress "the clinician must become a better scientist and the scientist a better clinician." Written by one who has impressive credentials for playing both roles, this volume on *Psychotherapy and the Modification of Abnormal Behavior* attempts to bridge, for the undergraduate reader, the chasm of background, interests, values, and orientation that too frequently sets researcher apart from clinician.

Hans Strupp is Professor of Psychology and Director of the Clinical Psychology Training Program at Vanderbilt University. He has held academic appointments at George Washington University and the University of North Carolina where he was Director of Psychological Services in the Department of Psychiatry of the University's Medical School.

He is a Diplomate in Clinical Psychology of the American Board of Professional Psychology, a Scientific Associate of the Academy of Psychoanalysis, a member of the American Academy of Psychotherapists and an editorial adviser to *Psychotherapy*, the *Journal of Consulting and Clinical Psychology*, and the *Journal of Nervous and Mental Disease*. He has authored more than ninety articles and reviews; several books devoted to psychotherapeutic research have been written or edited by him including *Psychotherapists in Action* (1960), *Research in Psychotherapy* (1962), and *Patients View Their Psychotherapy* (1969).

His recent critique, written in collaboration with Professor Allen E. Bergin, *Some Empirical and Conceptual Bases for Coordinated Research in Psychotherapy: A Critical Review of Issues, Trends, and Evidence*, when it appeared in the *International Journal of Psychiatry* in February 1969, was described by professional reviewers in terms such as these: "remarkably comprehensive, balanced . . . constructively critical . . . of major importance . . . essential reading for anyone devoted to psychotherapy research . . . the most authoritative, comprehensive and judicious of the many attempts to review this body of work . . . a tremendous service to the field."

The undergraduate reader, hopefully, will find evidence in this volume too of that compound of comprehensiveness, clarity, and fairness that has characterized Dr. Strupp's contributions to the study of psychotherapy.

Norman Garmezy

Preface

This book is an introduction to the field of psychotherapy—its theories and techniques, as well as to research and research problems in the area. The approach is novel, at least at the introductory level, but it is in keeping with the spirit of this series which is designed to acquaint the undergraduate student with the subject matter of particular areas of psychology and at the same time to expose him to the work of the researcher who devotes his energies to the systematic study of the phenomena in the domain.

Psychotherapy in the modern sense is less than a century old. Since the monumental discoveries of Breuer and Freud revolutionized man's thinking about emotional disturbances and their treatment, a voluminous literature has sprung up, the bulk of which is devoted to expositions of the theories of psychotherapy and, to a lesser extent, to descriptions of technique. The systematic and objective examination of the phenomena with which the psychotherapist deals in his daily work is of even more recent vintage. Research in psychotherapy is largely an American development which had its inception around 1940. Since that time the vast majority of studies have been contributed by English-speaking investigators, most of whom have had their training as clinical psychologists. Theory and practice, on the one hand, and research, on the other, have been largely divorced from each other, and only in the very recent past have there been signs of a growing rapprochement.

Originally defined as a medical (psychiatric) speciality, psychotherapy training used to be restricted to residents in psychiatry, although it could hardly be denied that psychotherapy employs psychological principles. However, there was considerable resistance to a full recognition of the fact that the scientific study of all psychological phenomena is the business of the psychologist whose training in research eminently qualifies him to carry forward such inquiries. Freud, though trained as a physician, was unequivocal in his assertion that psychoanalysis forms a part of psychology, not of medicine, and he felt very strongly that the advancement of the field as a science demanded free and open examination of the issues. Unfortunately, professional concerns and the formation of guilds impeded such inquiry for decades, and these forces have by no means disappeared. However, it is gratifying to note that many of the barriers are gradually being eroded, and the fresh air of unorthodoxy is beginning to sweep the scene. There is no question that the field will greatly benefit thereby in the years to come, even though many of the innovations which currently enjoy vogue may either disappear as fads or become absorbed in the mainstream of scientific and professional development.

With the rapid growth of the mental-health professions following World War II, psychologists began not only to bring psychotherapeutic phenomena under the magnifying glass of objective research, but, together with other nonmedical professionals (notably psychiatric social workers), acquired expertise in practicing psychotherapy. Training in psychotherapy since that time has become an integral part of graduate training for the clinical psychologist, and while most predoctoral programs provide instruction only at the journeyman level, many graduates usually seek further training and experience after leaving the university. The doctoral student commonly becomes acquainted with research in the area of psychotherapy. Upon graduation, compared with his colleague in psychiatry, his competence in research is typically greater, whereas the opposite holds true with respect to technical skills. The undergraduate student in psychology commonly learns a few facts about theories of psychotherapy—most textbooks in abnormal psychology devote relatively little space to it—but he learns virtually nothing about research in the area. It is this gap which the present text attempts to bridge. In this context it should also be mentioned that the "classical" model of psychotherapy, that of a 1-to-1 relationship between therapist and patient, has receded to the background, and is currently being superseded by group approaches, family therapy, and the like.

Most of the knowledge we possess in this area is the result of work by perceptive clinicians who have intensively worked with patients over long periods of time, and there is little doubt that their contributions to theory and technique far outdistance the efforts of the researcher, who, as I have noted, is very much a newcomer. As research in the area gradually got under way, many investigators were far better methodologists than clinicians, and their understanding of the phenomena they sought to investigate was often inadequate. These deficiencies are now being overcome, although it will undoubtedly take time.

Psychotherapy is very definitely a practical art and it is destined to remain so in the foreseeable future. This being the case, therapeutic skills cannot be learned from textbooks. They can only be acquired through prolonged apprenticeship, including close supervision. Mandatory, too, in my judgment, is thorough experience for the trainee in the patient role. This firsthand exposure to psychotherapy has usually been termed personal analysis or personal therapy. In short, no one should have any illusions that he can become a skilled psychotherapist in a few easy lessons. As a matter of fact, psychotherapy is exceedingly difficult to master, and we have as yet few criteria by which to evaluate the competence of a psychotherapist. Let it be clear that psychotherapy is a serious occupation which makes considerable demands on the therapist's emotional and intellectual resources. It requires a great deal of tact, patience, respect for the autonomy of other people, and—above all—absolute personal and professional integrity. It should never be forgotten that, as psychotherapists, we are dealing with unhappiness, suffering, and despair of our fellow men who grant us the rare privilege of sharing their innermost thoughts, feelings, and fantasies. It is our solemn responsibility to prove worthy of that trust.

What advantage might there accrue from combining theories and practical concerns with a consideration of the issues and problems confronting the researcher? My answer principally is that the research dimension adds perspective to the field. It highlights the tentativeness of all theoretical propositions; it underscores the enormous difficulties of making definitive assertions about virtually all aspects of the dynamic phenomena with which the therapist must be familiar; and it provides a healthy antidote to feelings of omniscience and omnipotence to which the therapist, more than any other professional person, is continually prone and which constitute a serious occupational hazard. By now, we know a fair amount about the psychological forces which complicate man's relationships with others and which have their roots in inner conflicts. However, our knowledge is rather modest compared to the sea of ignorance we glimpse as soon as we manage to divest ourselves of our complacency. Psychotherapy has a future as a scientific discipline to the extent that we are able to discern the limits of our present achievements. An appreciation of these facts, I trust, will foster a sense of humility.

Finally, I believe that the skills of the researcher are rather different from those of the clinician. In the past, the two have not communicated well, and they have often been distrustful of each other's work. Although separated by differences of temperament, ability, and *Weltanschauung*, they need to collaborate. They must learn from each other and such learning is bound to potentiate their respective efforts. I noted elsewhere that for the field to advance, the clinician must become a better scientist and the scientist a better clinician. The earlier such mutual understanding may be fostered in the student's career, the better.

This volume was written in response to an invitation from Dr. Norman Garmezy of the University of Minnesota. I am grateful to him for his continued encouragement and constructive criticism. Thanks are due Mr. Walter Maytham and McGraw-Hill Book Company for their patient support of this venture. To Mrs. Joan T. Reese I am indebted for typing numerous drafts of the manuscript. Finally, I have greatly benefited from my collaboration with Dr. Allen E. Bergin of Teachers College, Columbia University, with whom, during the last few years, I spent many hours exploring the frontiers of psychotherapy research. This work has broadened my perspective and deepened my thinking.

Hans H. Strupp

Contents

CHAPTER 1

PSYCHOTHERAPY: ART AND SCIENCE

This chapter presents an overview of the art and science of psychotherapy. Its purpose is to acquaint the reader with the process of psychotherapy, the work of the psychotherapist, and the kind of problems he seeks to solve. We shall also begin to consider the problems encountered by the investigator whose aim is to increase scientific understanding of psychotherapeutic phenomena. In order to appreciate the scientist's interests and goals in this area, it is first necessary to clarify the meaning of psychotherapy and the range of activities it encompasses.

What Is Psychotherapy?

As the name implies, *psychotherapy* refers to treatment by psychological means, but the literal meaning of the term is more likely to confuse than to illuminate. Furthermore, commonly used terms like *doctor, patient, treatment,* and *cure* strongly suggest that psychotherapy is a form of *medical* treatment whose goal is to improve the recipient's "mental health." As we shall see, these terms have important historical roots, but their present-day utility is slight. While no definition of psychotherapy is universally accepted, it is important to note at the outset that the psychotherapist's activities differ distinctly from those of the physician: the patient's role in psychotherapy is only remotely related to that of the medical patient; the kinds of disorders for which individuals seek help are not diseases as usually understood; the treatment is unlike any medical treatment; and the meaning of the term *mental health* is extremely fuzzy. If the disease model is not applicable to psychotherapy, what alternatives are available? Before we attempt to answer this question it may prove helpful to sketch briefly the transactions occurring between a psychotherapist and his patient. (While potentially misleading, terms like *patient* and *therapist* have become so firmly entrenched that it would be awkward to replace them.)

CASE HISTORY

Joe M, age twenty-seven, consults a physician and complains of recurring headaches, insomnia, occasional fainting spells, and vague feelings of anxiety and depression. The doctor performs a physical examination, conducts a variety of tests, and ultimately informs him that he can not find any organic basis for the difficulties. However, he learns in the course of the consultation that Mr. M "works too hard," "drives himself," frequently quarrels with his wife and his employer, and in general appears none too happy. Being psychologically minded, he attributes Mr. M's troubles to emotional factors and calls his symptoms *psychogenic* (i.e., originating "in the mind"). Furthermore, since he is not fond of prescribing tranquilizing drugs in situations of this kind, he informs the patient that he might benefit from psychotherapy and refers him to a psychotherapist [who may be a psychiatrist, psychoanalyst, clinical psychologist, or psychiatric social worker (see Glossary for definitions)]. Depending on his sophistication, Mr. M may conclude that the physician has politely informed him that (1) as there is nothing wrong with him, the symptoms being all "in his mind," he is a hypochondriac and perhaps malingering; (2) he is "crazy" or "going crazy"; or (3) (more correctly) his symptoms are caused by emotions of which he is unaware and over which he has no control.

Let us assume that Mr. M is sufficiently bothered by his difficulties to want relief and that he is not overly concerned about the adverse connotations of consulting a psychiatrist. The stipulation that the patient is motivated for psychotherapy will be seen as quite important. To simplify the discussion let us assume, too, that the specialist he is consulting confines his practice to psychotherapy. After a certain amount of hesitation, Mr. M arranges an appointment with Dr. L.

Not knowing what to expect, Mr. M is understandably anxious as he enters the therapist's office, which has the appearance of a fairly comfortable living room. Having been invited to sit down and asked "What brings you here?" he tells Dr. L much the same story as he had told his physician, adding, "Can you help me?"

Depending on a variety of factors which need not concern us at this point, the therapist may tentatively answer the patient's question by saying, "Many patients with problems similar to yours have been helped by psychotherapy." He may suggest that they meet a specified number of times per week, each session comprising fifty minutes. Invariably the matter of the therapist's fee will be discussed. For the rest, the situation is left largely unstructured, and the patient is given to understand that the time is essentially his to do with as he pleases and that the therapist will listen carefully and attentively but must rely on the patient to provide raw material for their conversations. The patient is also told that he is free to say what he pleases and indeed encouraged to do so. Thus the patient has entered psychotherapy.

As time goes on, patient and therapist continue to meet until they agree to terminate, usually by mutual consent. Their main activity is talk, of which the patient does by far the larger amount. At times, the therapist asks a question, offers a comment, or gives an interpretation. The therapist never gives the patient a physical examination, does not prescribe medications, and rarely if ever offers advice.

What kind of treatment is this? What is the nature of the disease being treated? What manner of doctor is the therapist? How can a person who actively participates in his treatment and collaborates with the therapist be properly called a "patient"? What sort of cure can one expect? These are some of the important questions which laymen, patients, therapists, and scientists wish to know more about. As Einstein (1936) remarked: "The whole of science is nothing more than a refinement of everyday thinking."

HOW PSYCHOTHERAPY DIFFERS FROM MEDICAL TREATMENT

While the foregoing description of the therapeutic process gives the superficial appearance of great simplicity, in reality we are dealing with exceedingly complicated and intricate phenomena, which, for the most part, are not nearly as well understood as we would like. The task of the scientist is to contribute to a better understanding of the phenomena in nature, whether they involve physical, chemical, or biological forces or whether they center around human relationships, as does psychotherapy. Whatever else psychotherapy may do, it prominently involves a *human relationship*, and it is partly this relationship which is hypothesized to have therapeutic value.

To be sure, medical treatment (unless the patient is unconscious on the operating table and a complete "object" to the surgeon) also entails a human relationship between patient and physician, but it is generally considered secondary or subsidiary to the actual therapy, which may be physical, surgical, pharmacological, etc.

Many physicians are aware that a sizable proportion of the patients who consult them for supposedly medical problems are helped more effectively by reassurance, a friendly word from the doctor, and anything that might boost their morale. Hence the importance of the physician's bedside manner has long been stressed, and in many cases it may be a more potent medicine than any drug he may prescribe. Similarly, physicians recognize that the value of any drug may be considerably enhanced by the curative power the patient (or his doctor) attributes to it. This is the so-called placebo effect (a *placebo* is a sugar pill or any other inert substance), about which more will be said. To the extent that the physician succeeds in reassuring the patient or bolstering his morale, he is engaging in a form of psychotherapy which has been practiced over the centuries, but one which overlaps only slightly the role and function of the modern psychotherapist. Nevertheless, some writers (Frank, 1961) regard the psychotherapist's influence as largely synonymous with that of the mental or spiritual healer. Arguing against this assertion is the fact that the physician or anyone else who functions in the mental healer role is proceeding quite intuitively, and he is usually not interested in attempting to specify the kind of psychological influence he exerts on the patient. Be that as it may, the physician's concern is primarily with the body as a physicochemical machine, and his relationship with the patient as a person is usually incidental, although the dividing line is admittedly anything but clear. His training comprises the search for causes of malfunctions in the body (diagnosis) and the correction, amelioration, or control of any malfunction he has detected.

NEUROSIS AS A PROBLEM IN LIVING

But what are the malfunctions or diseases with which the psychotherapist is concerned? In common parlance, these are referred to as *nervousness, nervous breakdown, nervous and mental disease* (an obsolete term which was common in the nineteenth century), *psychoneurosis*, and the like. What kinds of diseases are these?

As we saw, Mr. M was suffering, in part, from physical symptoms, but his physician could not find anything organically wrong with the patient; that is, he attributed his difficulties to emotional causes which he did not view as the proper domain of medicine, and hence he referred them to a psychotherapist. To be sure, he might have prescribed one of the numerous tranquilizers, as is frequently done by physicians today, but he realized that the predominant effect of such medications is to dull symptoms such as anxiety, although, like aspirin, they often produce quite impressive temporary relief. Furthermore, he believed that this particular patient should seek a more radical cure, that is, a form of treatment designed to deal more effectively with the underlying causes, which somehow he perceived in the totality of the patient's life, notably in his relationships with important people in his life.

It requires no specialized knowledge to appreciate the fact that mental events often influence the functioning of the body and vice versa. An actor anticipating opening night often experiences stage fright, which may be accompanied by palpitations of the heart, shallow breathing, sweating, diarrhea, and the like. Conversely, similar symptoms can be produced by injecting adrenaline into a person's bloodstream. Physicians specializing in psychosomatic medicine, which attempts to solve the age-old mind-body problem by recognizing the importance of interactions between physical manifestations and mental events, may treat a condition like stomach ulcer by pharmacological or surgical means, but on other occasions they may counsel a patient to seek the help of a psychotherapist to help him change his outlook on life. The point to be made is that psychological factors may have a pervasive influence on the functioning of the body, but if these factors are subsumed under the heading of psychoneurosis or neurosis (which are identical terms), as is frequently done, we have not added to our understanding of the disease process. The answer obviously must lie elsewhere.

It appears more fruitful to view the processes with which the psychotherapist is concerned, not as disease entities, but as problems in living. The individual who is suffering from emotional problems, by and large, is an unhappy person, although he may not admit the unhappiness to himself. Like Mr. M, he may experience anxiety, depression, and a host of physical symptoms, but none of the symptoms in and of itself constitutes a neurosis. In other instances, the person may experience no clearly definable symptoms, but he will perceive within himself a sense of emptiness, futility, and a lack of meaning in his life. In still other cases, he may engage in actions which are socially disapproved; he may make excessive use of drugs, alcohol, etc.; he may get married and divorced frequently; and he may be unstable in other respects. Thus, it becomes clear that any effort to define neurosis as a form of physical disease (in the medical sense) encounters serious difficulties.

If neurosis is not a physical disease, perhaps it is a disease of the mind? This alternative has traditionally been followed by psychiatry (a medical specialty devoted to the diagnosis and treatment of mental disorders), and it still represents the view of many physicians and laymen. Proceeding in this direction, one might engage in the following metaphorical reasoning: Diseases of the mind are *like* diseases of the body, and a sickness of the mind has a *cause*, which must be diagnosed and treated like physical disease. In this sense Hamlet was sick and a person who cannot get along with his wife is also sick; however, the term *sick* has no precise meaning here. It is a figure of speech to be taken no more literally than a poetic comparison of a lover to a flower. Basically, there is nothing wrong with metaphors provided the analogy is not accepted as immutable reality. Yet this has occurred in the mental health field. Mental disease is conceptualized, diagnosed, and treated as analogous to physical disease, and physical health serves as the model for mental health. As Szasz (1961), one of the major spokesmen for the view that contemporary concepts of mental health and disease are a myth, has convincingly shown, this kind of labeling has been of great significance historically because it permitted persons who in the Middle Ages were accused of practicing witchcraft or having traffic with the Devil to be treated as sick people. This redefinition from *sinner* to *patient* led to more humane treatment on the part of society and paved the way to significant advances in the wake of a growing awareness that however mental disease is defined, we are dealing with serious social problems.

THE ROLE AND FUNCTION OF THE PSYCHOTHERAPIST

However, there are other implications which are partly responsible for the lingering confusion about the role and function of the modern psychotherapist. With the definition of the sufferer as a patient in need of treatment, the gamut of human problems became the concern of medicine, and thus the physician emerged as the person properly qualified to treat them. By this reasoning, unhappiness, marital disharmony, inability to get along with one's boss or spouse, conflicts about the choice of vocation, and many other difficulties modern man encounters in adjusting to life in a complex world have been labeled as medical problems. Since society has delegated the responsibility for diagnosing and treating medical problems to physicians, until fairly recently only a doctor of medicine was considered qualified to treat neuroses and related disorders, or, minimally, such "treatment" had to be carried out under medical supervision. This is an instance in which the needs of the patient have become intertwined with aspirations of a profession to extend its power and sphere of influence.

Broadly speaking, then, the psychotherapist is a professional whose subject matter is man's relations with himself and his peers; his struggles to become an autonomous, independent, and responsible member of society; and the inner difficulties he encounters in becoming a person who lives up to his potential, exercises his talents, and creates a place for himself in the world. In this vein, Harry Stack Sullivan, a prominent American psychiatrist, defined psychiatry as the study of interpersonal relations. If this definition is accepted, the work of the modern psychotherapist is closer to that of the sociologist, the psychologist, and the anthropologist than it is to the physician. Further, as a behavioral scientist he is far removed from the theologian, whose ultimate concern is man's relations with God.

By this time the reader has undoubtedly wondered about the multitude of patients confined to mental hospitals or similar institutions (in the United States the census of mental-hospital patients exceeds 1 million). Surely, persons who engage in bizarre behavior, admit to "hearing voices," assert to be important historical personages, or cannot get along in society must be called "sick"? As has already been indicated, the problems of mental normality and abnormality and their counterparts mental health and sickness are exceedingly complex (volumes in this series deal extensively with this topic). For present purposes it is sufficient to note that there are indeed diseases of the brain and the central nervous system which may be caused by infections or hereditary factors and which may lead to disturbances in man's reasoning, feelings, and emotions. Similarly, so-called functional mental disorders (defined by the absence of a known organic basis) may in part be the product of biochemical or metabolic malfunctions, concerning which more has been learned in recent years. Such disorders are the proper concern of the physician and the psychiatrist; however, to the extent that these patients are also suffering from the adverse effects of a broken home, a deprived childhood, and deficiencies in socialization, their problems fall within the province of psychotherapy regardless of whether psychotherapeutic help is available to them, which all too often it is not.[*]

The Work of the Psychotherapist

THE PSYCHOTHERAPIST AS A SPECIALIST IN HUMAN COMMUNICATION

Having established that the psychotherapist is basically a psychological specialist, we need to examine more closely *what* he does, *how* he does it, and the manner in which he accounts for (explains) his activities. While psychotherapy takes many different forms, and while there are many theories of psychotherapy, all psychotherapists deal with the problem of change in personality and behavior, including feelings, emotions, attitudes, and actions. Ideally, the psychotherapist wishes to help patients who desire change, and his work is designed to help the patient accomplish whatever changes he wishes to make; that is, he greatly prefers to work with individuals who seek his services, freely consent to work with him, and consult him for problems which they experience as troublesome. This wording serves to underscore the disinclination of most psychotherapists to change anyone against his will or to work with individuals whose treatment is desired by a spouse, employer, parent, or by a court of law. Like the attorney, the psychotherapist represents his client's interests and no one else's. The therapist's goal is the client's *autonomy* and *independence,* and, like a wise parent, he aspires to see the child (patient) grow up, become a mature adult, and take care of himself. Conversely, he assumes that the patient is suffering because he has somehow failed to realize these goals on his own. In an important sense, therefore, he construes the patient's problems in terms of immaturity, dependence, lack of competence, and ignorance.

[*] Schizophrenia, one of the major psychoses, is a good example of a disorder characterized by a complex interplay of biochemical and psychological factors. While much remains to be learned about schizophrenia, it is likely that certain experiences in early childhood, especially destructive attitudes on the part of the mother, may trigger biochemical mechanisms in individuals whose heredity predisposes them, thus producing in later life the clinical syndrome of a serious mental disorder.

The patient is sick because his past experience has not properly equipped him to cope with life's problems as the adult encounters them in this culture. Stated slightly differently, he either has not learned to cope effectively or he has acquired faulty techniques whose end results are the kinds of problems which led Mr. M to consult a physician. The psychotherapist proceeds on the assumption that all human behavior (or at least the kind he has any hope of modifying) is the product of past experience; that is, he deals with *learned* behavior. Just as a person has learned his native tongue and acquired a multitude of cognitive and motor skills, he has also learned ways and means (techniques and strategies) of getting along with his fellows, dominating them, doing their bidding, following their example, and cooperating with them. Usually, he cannot delineate these strategies any more than he can explicate the rules of grammar inherent in his native tongue, but his conduct is governed by certain rules in similar ways. In terms of contemporary computer terminology, we might say that the person has been "programmed" by his past experience to behave more or less consistently, but we must infer the nature of the program from his behavior; the program is not available from punch cards.

Following this analogy, an important aspect of the psychotherapist's task is to determine the nature of the patient's programs—that is, the beliefs, assumptions, and hypotheses he entertains about his behavior as well as that of others—and to bring these programs to the patient's attention in the hope that greater self-awareness will lead to the kinds of changes he desires.

From a somewhat different standpoint, the patient is suffering from problems in the area of *self-control,* which he construes as helplessness. His complaints (symptoms) take this form: "I would like to live in harmony with my wife, but contrary to what I want, we seem to be fighting all the time." Or: "Whenever I have to make a speech in public, I become uncontrollably anxious so that often I avoid these situations, much as I realize that in order to get ahead in my work this kind of activity is highly desirable." Or: "I get so depressed at times that I just want to crawl in a hole. I cannot do anything about it." Or: "I don't know what has come over me, but I have to wash my hands a dozen times a day." Thus the patient acknowledges the existence of inner forces over which he feels he has no control, but which he believes he should be able to control. The psychotherapist's goal, therefore, is to help the patient increase his radius of independent action. Essentially, he translates the patient's assertion "I can't" to "I don't want to" and inquires why the patient might not want to do the things he allegedly is intent upon doing. He concedes the reality to the patient's conflict but questions the adequacy of the patient's formulation of the problem.

The psychotherapist, therefore, is a specialist in human learning and the rules which govern the acquisition (and conversely, extinction) of behavior. But he is also a specialist in understanding and decoding human communications which often take exceedingly complicated and intricate forms. The problem in part lies in the fact that man typically does not make simple responses to specific stimuli but creates and responds to complex symbols, of which he may have only a dim understanding. For example, a man may harbor the belief (of which he is unaware) that women are dangerous. For purposes of this illustration it is not necessary to examine how he acquired this belief, but it can be seen that it will affect his relationships with women in particular ways. Specifically, such a belief will result in his avoiding members of the female sex; this, however, is neither possible nor is it in accordance with his erotic strivings toward members of the opposite sex. While this example represents a considerable oversimplification, it conveys the point that the man in this example finds himself in a conflict. He *wants* to be close to women, but something within him warns him of (admittedly unrealistic) danger. Until he becomes deeply convinced that his fears are indeed groundless, his life will be unduly complicated. Adding to this difficulty is the human propensity to hide unpleasant truths from oneself, a subject to which Sigmund Freud made lasting contributions. Some beliefs, such as the above, may strike the laymen as nonsensical and even fantastic, yet everyone has had experience with nightmares and dreams which often contain elements (albeit in highly disguised form) of fantasies which form an integral part of every person's mental life and in some cases profoundly influence feelings, emotions, attitudes, and actions.

The preceding exposition assumes that man's observable behavior, particularly in his relations with other people, is governed by *central* processes which lend it stability and consistency. It is this kind of stability, commonly referred to as *personality* or *character*, which makes it possible to anticipate or predict (within limits) how a given person will behave under given circumstances. All of us are able to make such predictions about persons with whom we have had a close relationship. The view that mental life is governed by forces only some of which are available to man's conscious awareness is called the *psychodynamic* standpoint, which is widely though not universally accepted. This approach contrasts most sharply, as we shall see, with the behavioristic position, whose proponents reject dynamic processes and attempt to explain behavior in terms of the principles of learning (see Chapter 4).

HOW THE PSYCHOTHERAPIST HELPS

In general terms, the activities of the psychotherapist may be described as falling into three areas which in practice are closely interrelated: (1) he engages in an interpersonal relationship with the patient; (2) he attempts to understand the patient's communications (which are largely verbal but also include body movements, gestures, and the like); (3) he communicates understanding to the patient at appropriate times and in other ways attempts to influence the patient's beliefs, attitudes, feelings, and actions. These aspects of the work add up to a significant emotional experience for the patient which mediates *experiential* learning. It is not sufficient for the psychotherapist to inform the patient that he harbors an unrealistic belief or that he misconstrues reality in other ways—if this were the case, psychotherapy would be considerably simpler than it ordinarily is—but the patient must assimilate the new understanding and make it his own. Just as a printed menu is no substitute for the experience of eating a meal, informing the patient that he engages in self-defeating behavior or supplying him with possible reasons through explanations or interpretations does not change it. The importance of the patient's *emotional experience* in psychotherapy cannot be overemphasized, and it accounts in part for the long period of time usually required for psychotherapy.

The psychotherapeutic relationship resembles other human relationships, notably those between expert and client, teacher and pupil, master and apprentice, but it is radically different in significant respects. Superficially, it appears to be a relationship between adults, one of whom is ostensibly providing a service that the other is receiving. Thus, the outer structure of the therapeutic relationship is that of a business or contractual relationship, but these considerations are overshadowed by other factors.

The therapist's attitude is businesslike, respectful, objective, and friendly. He assures the patient of neutrality and strict confidentiality, he views his relationship to the patient as a means to an end, and he is mindful of the fact that the patient is one of many patients he sees every day. For him, psychotherapy is a business or profession which permits him to earn a living, although it provides him with job satisfactions which are a "fringe benefit" for most people; and since he does not see the therapeutic relationship as an analogue to friendship, he can view the patient with a fair degree of dispassionateness and detachment, which are important assets in his work. Like any self-respecting professional, he is desirous of doing a good job, and he lives up to his obligations toward the patient by being punctual and reliable in keeping appointments. Most important, during each therapeutic hour he bends his energies to the task of listening to and understanding the patient's communications to the exclusion of any personal preoccupations. Sensitivity, tact, and empathy help him in this endeavor. His appreciation of the fact that the patient often suffers and continues to be unhappy, however, does not detract him from his primary goal of helping the patient to become an autonomous adult. Since this aspect of the therapeutic enterprise is frequently misunderstood, some persons consider psychotherapy as equivalent to the purchase of friendship. To be sure, the psychotherapist is not a paragon of virtue any more than any other mortal, and he will have personal feelings and reactions to the patient which at times may be troublesome, but he must guard against these to the best of his ability. Just as a lawyer or a physician may get entangled in the personal affairs of his client or patient, the psychotherapist runs similar risks (which, as a matter of fact, are incomparably greater), but if he succumbs to them, he has abdicated his role as a psychotherapist. Thus, from the therapist's standpoint the therapeutic relationship is basically an impersonal relationship, although the framework appears to be conducive to a highly personal one.

How does the situation appear from the patient's vantage point? First, it must be remembered that he is distressed and keenly desirous of help and relief. He has been told that the therapist will respect his confidences; that talking about his difficulties is likely to help; and that he can talk about anything and express any feeling without evoking criticism or endangering the relationship. However, he must accept these assurances on faith since he has no way of ascertaining their truth until he has put them to the test. He has also been told that psychotherapy is a collaborative venture which depends heavily upon his cooperation. While the therapist typically makes no specific promises, the patient hopes that by following the "rules" he will feel better. Indeed, the beginning of therapy often engenders a sense of relief, and improvements are not uncommon. (At mental hygiene clinics, where the preponderant majority of patients are nowadays treated, psychotherapy frequently terminates at this point, and some 75 percent of the patients feel "improved," at least for the time being.) This may occur after ten, fifteen, or twenty-five hours, and the outcome of psychotherapy is frequently measured in terms of this relatively brief exposure. Long-term, intensive psychotherapy, often described as *psychoanalysis*, is a much rarer occurrence and is almost entirely restricted to affluent patients who can pay the fees of a private practitioner over periods of time ranging from one to three years or even longer.

THE ESSENCE OF PSYCHOTHERAPY

We have seen that psychotherapy consists of a human relationship which serves as a vehicle for producing changes in the client's personality or behavior. Like any good human relationship it is characterized by openness and trust, but the fact that it is also a professional relationship in which an expert provides a service to a client who pays for the service sets it apart from any other human relationship. As one writer put it, it is a highly personal relationship within an impersonal framework. The nature of the transactions between therapist and patient, the character of the problem for which help is sought, the kinds of changes to be effected, and the optimal strategies for effecting them—these are the major topics with which the various theories of psychotherapy are concerned. A theory of psychotherapy, like any theory, attempts to deal in a parsimonious way with a set of complex phenomena, and it serves as a tool for ordering and operating upon them. The existence of so many, and sharply divergent, theories points to significant gaps in our knowledge relative to the phenomena the theory is trying to explain. The problem is further complicated by the fact that since in psychotherapy we are not dealing with impersonal forces like gravity or energy but with social and psychological arrangements among people, including their attitudes, values, and beliefs, any theory of psychotherapy inevitably tells us something about the author's conceptions of the nature of man and man's place in the world. Thus, theories of psychotherapy subtly shade into philosophy, political ideology, and sociology. They deal with conceptions of freedom and control, and the goals of psychotherapy are thoroughly intertwined with the role and function a given society prescribes for the well-functioning person. Therefore, the practice of psychotherapy and its underlying theories are uniquely sensitive to the prevailing social climate and may indeed be largely determined by it. A sharp clash, for example, may be observed between psychotherapy in the Western world and in Soviet Russia, although in our more permissive laissez faire society divergent theories of psychotherapy can exist side by side. Nevertheless, the social climate has a strong influence on fads and fashions in psychotherapy anywhere.

Be that as it may, psychotherapy is basically a process of learning new techniques for getting along with one's contemporaries and modifying those strategies which are shown to be maladaptive or self-defeating. In this sense, psychotherapy is often described as a process of reeducation, after-education, or simply education. Unlike any other educational experience, however, the subject matter is not a cognitive content (like French, Latin, or any other subject taught in school) nor is it a motor skill (like ice skating, piano playing, or typing); the subject matter consists of the strategies, attitudes, feelings, and behaviors one employs in interpersonal relations. Another difference is the modification of techniques which are already in the patient's behavioral repertoire; consequently, therapeutic learning is corrective learning (although admittedly some learning is quite new). Finally, and perhaps most important, the relationship between patient and therapist serves to make explicit the troublesome aspects of the patient's interpersonal techniques. In later chapters, three prominent theories will be reviewed: (1) psychoanalysis; (2) client-centered therapy; and (3) behavior therapy. While these theories are broadly representative of contemporary views, they are in no way exhaustive. Harper (1959) delineated thirty-six systems, and even that list is not complete. In the final analysis, there are probably as many systems of psychotherapy as there are psychotherapists, but many variations are minor and need not be considered by the reader.

The Role of the Researcher-Scientist

Regardless of theoretical differences, it is clear that psychotherapy is an applied art and the psychotherapist is an applied scientist. In the same way the physician applies principles of biochemistry, anatomy, physiology, etc., and the engineer relies on the laws of physics, the psychotherapist utilizes psychological principles. Therefore, the science basic to psychotherapy is psychology. (Psychiatry, too, is an applied science although in some respects it may be viewed as a basic science.) The psychotherapist tailors basic psychological principles to the problems of the individual patient and, at least in principle (although not always in practice), the psychotherapist is aware of these principles and can specify them. This ability to make explicit the nature of his operations also sets the psychotherapist apart from other mental healers who employ psychological principles but who do so intuitively and unsystematically.

What, then, is the role and function of the scientist-researcher-investigator in psychotherapy? Generally speaking, the researcher in psychotherapy, like any scientist, is concerned with the advancement of knowledge. In this case, his objective is to contribute to an improved understanding of the psychological principles underlying psychological change; however, in addition to his interest in basic psychological principles he is equally concerned with the applications of these principles which he hopes will be translated by the psychotherapist into more effective practice.

In order to appreciate more fully the researcher's role in psychotherapy, it is important to keep in mind that virtually all significant advances in this area, which were initiated by Freud's monumental discoveries toward the end of the last century, have been made by practicing psychotherapists, that is, clinicians whose work centers around the task of helping patients solve their problems in living.

From this work with individual patients they distilled the principles and developed the theories which constitute the fund of knowledge available today. These contributors were not scientists who isolated phenomena in the laboratory and manipulated them experimentally, as the physicist or the chemist would do; instead they dealt with the complexity represented by the person who approaches the psychotherapist for help. As a result, there are to be found many assertions and formulations in the field which are based largely on clinical observations and which have not been adequately tested and documented. The task of specifying, documenting, and testing these clinical insights falls to the psychotherapy researcher, who came upon the scene barely a quarter of a century ago. The researcher in this area is usually a psychologist, although psychiatrists, sociologists, and other behavioral scientists are also making important contributions. Beginning in the 1950s, and increasingly since around 1960, research in psychotherapy has gained increasing momentum, as evidenced in part by the steep rise in the number of publications which have appeared since that time.

HOW EFFECTIVE IS PSYCHOTHERAPY?

As soon as the practice of psychotherapy became a professional activity around the turn of the century, questions began to be raised about its effectiveness, and controversies sprang up which are still rampant. In its traditional form, the question "Is psychotherapy effective?" has scant meaning and is on a par with the question "Is education effective?" or "Is internal medicine effective?" The logical and common-sense answer is (or should be) "It depends." Once the reasonableness of this qualified answer is admitted, one begins to appreciate the researcher's job in the area. The researcher attempts to specify the conditions under which a particular set of therapeutic interventions leads to a given result, and he tries to determine which characteristics of the patient and therapist, which qualities of their interaction, and what environmental circumstances bring about that result.

An analogy will clarify the point. If one wishes to assess whether a college education is effective, one must specify what is meant by "effectiveness." Does it make the graduate a better or happier person than he otherwise would be? Does it enable him to get a better job?

Does it make the student more educated? In short, one must first define the *criteria* one is willing to accept as evidence of a desirable outcome. In psychotherapy research, the need for a consensus on outcome has been appreciated only in recent years. Previously, to one person "improvement" meant that the patient felt better, to another that he lost a particular symptom, to a third that he functioned more effectively in interpersonal situations, and so on. If one wishes to assess therapeutic outcomes in terms of mental health, he must define what he understands by this criterion. Until such time as therapists, investigators, and the public agree on a definition, figures of "percent improvement" which have been common in older tabulations are largely meaningless.

Next, one must define the process to which one wishes to attribute a particular outcome. To return to the analogy, a college education is composed of many ingredients—courses, instructors, fellow students, fraternity life, and so on. Even if one attempts to assess the effectiveness of a single course, one must describe precisely the instructor's technique, which is in turn intertwined with his interest in the subject matter, enthusiasm for teaching, interest in a particular student, and so on. Similarly, in psychotherapy one must specify not only the techniques a therapist uses, but one must study his personality and attitudes, goals, values, and many other factors. Moreover, one must examine and assess the teacher's interaction with particular students and their characteristics and attitudes. In many studies purportedly evaluating the effectiveness of psychotherapy or comparing the relative merits of different methods, such specifications typically have not been made, which constitutes a serious omission.

Finally, the value of instructional techniques must be judged in relation to the students' preparation, personality, motivation, interest, and other characteristics. It is pointless to study the effectiveness of a course in calculus, no matter how skillfully it may be taught or how much dedication the teacher may bring to his subject matter, unless the student has the requisite background and his level of intelligence is sufficiently high. If one were to select a random sample of students whose IQ varied between say 75 and 150, one would expect to find that the highly intelligent students would do very well whereas dull members of the sample would achieve unimpressive results. If one averaged their performance, the results might also be disappointing. In psychotherapy the situation is not too dissimilar if one fails to pay close attention to the characteristics of the patient, the nature and severity of his difficulties, their persistence, his motivation for change, and a host of other variables whose importance is increasingly being recognized.

It is apparent, then, that in the absence of the foregoing specifications one cannot begin to approach the question of whether psychotherapy is effective. Any study therefore must be carefully scrutinized to determine the extent to which the investigator has controlled for the multitude of variables which must not be left to vary freely if the comparison aspires to meaningfulness. Today there are no studies which approximate closely these stipulations, although there is abundant clinical evidence that an appreciable number of patients who are selected for a particular form of psychotherapy benefit from the experience; but it is only fair to concede that for many others it seems to provide little help. Furthermore, every form of psychotherapy appears to have its share of successes and failures. What complicates the evaluative task so tremendously is the fact that many variables which have been briefly mentioned *interact* in unknown ways, sometimes facilitating, sometimes impeding each other, and rigorous controls which are an important requirement in any scientific study are extraordinarily difficult to achieve. The reason is that human beings, unlike laboratory animals, cannot be isolated from a host of extraneous influences whose possible effects must be weighed against the work of the psychotherapist.

The technical and methodological problems facing the researcher will be considered in greater detail in subsequent chapters. For the present it is sufficient to record that they are formidable, which largely accounts for the slow progress many observers have noted and which has led others to become deeply disillusioned about the prospects. Finally, the researcher is not only concerned with the problem of outcome, but he also wishes to guide the searchlight of scientific inquiry to a host of other questions as well. However, in the final analysis his focus rests on the question: What set of technical operations lead to given psychological changes under specified conditions?

Summary

Psychotherapy has been defined as the planful application of psychological techniques for the purpose of inducing personality and behavior change. It is an applied behavioral science, and while it has its roots in medicine and psychiatry, it cannot properly be regarded as a form of medical treatment. Indeed, medical analogies are considered misleading. Psychotherapy is concerned with personality and behavior change, not with the cure of disease. The problems with which the psychotherapist deals are problems in living and, more particularly, problems people encounter in their interpersonal relations. Psychotherapy can only modify learned behavior or the strategies which people habitually employ in dealing with their fellows. Thus psychotherapy is essentially an educational process, and the psychotherapist's work approximates more closely that of a teacher than that of a physician.

The psychotherapist (1) provides the patient with an interpersonal relationship which is conducive to a corrective emotional experience, and (2) employs the relationship as a vehicle for technical interventions which differ in terms of divergent theoretical assumptions. The psychotherapist is an expert in understanding human communications, especially disguised messages, and his goal is to help the patient achieve greater autonomy and independence.

There are many theories of psychotherapy, often characterized by marked disagreements. Theories of psychotherapy, at least in part, deal with the nature of man and his place in the world, and they are sensitive to the prevailing social climate.

The psychotherapist, as an applied scientist, collaborates with the researcher, whose emphasis rests upon expanding knowledge concerning the basic phenomena of psychological change. The researcher's task is to document and specify clinical insights the psychotherapist obtains through his work with individual patients and to explain these insights in terms of common psychological principles. Despite differing emphases, the scientist and the practitioner share common goals.

The investigation of psychotherapy presents great technical and methodological difficulties which have only recently begun to be scrutinized. Until greater specification of the phenomena can be achieved, it is meaningless to compare different forms of psychotherapy or to evaluate the effectiveness of psychotherapy "in general."

Suggested Readings

BROMBERG, W. *The mind of man: A history of psychotherapy and psychoanalysis.* New York: Harper & Row, 1959.

FORD, D. H., & URBAN, H. B. *Systems of psychotherapy.* New York: Wiley, 1963.

FRANK, J. D. *Persuasion and healing: A comparative study of psychotherapy.* Baltimore: Johns Hopkins, 1961.

FREUD, S. *An outline of psychoanalysis.* New York: Norton, 1949.

FROMM, E. *Man for himself.* New York: Rinehart, 1947.

FROMM-REICHMANN, F. *Principles of intensive psychotherapy.* Chicago: University of Chicago, 1950.

GILL, M. M., NEWMAN, R., & REDLICH, F. C. *The initial interview in psychiatric practice.* New York: International Universities, 1954.

HARPER, R. A. *Psychoanalysis and psychotherapy: 36 systems.* Englewood Cliffs, N.J.: Prentice-Hall, 1959.

JOINT COMMISSION ON MENTAL ILLNESS AND HEALTH. *Action for mental health.* New York: Basic Books, 1961.

REIK, T. *Listening with the third ear.* New York: Farrar, Straus, 1949.

SULLIVAN, H. S. *The psychiatric interview.* New York: Norton, 1954.

SZASZ, T. S. *The ethics of psychoanalysis.* New York: Basic Books, 1965.

WOLBERG, L. R. *The technique of psychotherapy.* New York: Grune & Stratton, 1967.

CHAPTER 2

PSYCHOANALYTIC
PSYCHOTHERAPY

Modern psychotherapy begins with the discoveries of Sigmund Freud, whose insights revolutionized conceptions of mental disorder and normality, led to a coherent theory of personality development, and gave rise to a technique for dealing with man's neurotic problems. The influence of Freud's thought has extended far beyond psychology and psychiatry into anthropology, literature, religion, and art. In short, whatever criticisms may be leveled at his theories, few men have had a greater impact on Western civilization in the twentieth century.

In the present context we shall be concerned primarily with those aspects of Freud's formulations which have a direct bearing on the theory and practice of psychotherapy. Other volumes in this series deal with psychoanalysis as a theory of personality and abnormal behavior.

Background

In the early 1880s, while working in the laboratory of the physiologist Brücke, in Vienna, Sigmund Freud (1856–1939) made the acquaintance of a respected physician, Joseph Breuer (1842–1925), who was attending a young woman patient suffering from hysteria. She had fallen ill during a period of stress, when she was nursing her sick father. The disturbance manifested itself through numerous symptoms, including anesthesia of her right arm and leg, restrictions of her field of vision, difficulty in recognizing people, etc. Her condition had grown progressively worse. Breuer made the observation that when he hypnotized his patient, who under the pseudonym "Miss Anna O." achieved fame in the annals of psychoanalysis, she was able to recall experiences and events of which she was unaware during her waking state. Furthermore, the feelings she experienced in connection with these events were as vivid as they were painful. When Breuer succeeded in evoking these feelings, which seemed to go back to painful memories, and in inducing his patient to express them, he found that she was greatly relieved upon awakening from her hypnotic state. Repeated application of this technique resulted in marked improvement, which turned out to be lasting. The "talking cure," as Anna O. called it, had been born.

While there is a great distance between this case history and modern psychoanalytic psychotherapy, several important insights had been gained: (1) There evidently was a relationship between hysterical symptoms and hypnosis. (2) Feelings of which the patient was unaware and which she could not express in the waking state could be brought to awareness during hypnosis; that is, they were previously unconscious but continued to exert an influence on the patient's mental life. (3) There was some relationship between painful feelings and hysterical symptoms, and the expression of these feelings led to a diminution of the symptom. (4) There apparently was a force within the patient that pushed these feelings out of awareness (subsequently called *repression*). (5) Similarly, there had to be a barrier in the patient's mind that kept these feelings from becoming conscious (that is, there were *defenses* against painful feelings, which showed themselves as a seemingly paradoxical *resistance* to cure). (6) These forces are pitted against each other, giving rise to an *intrapsychic conflict*. (7) Painful feelings, if denied proper expression, can be converted into physical symptoms (hence the term *conversion reaction*), and this process is reversible, as was true under hypnotic treatment. (8) The patient's relationship to the doctor was important in effecting a cure.

This last factor was not given much prominence in Breuer's first account—beyond the implied statement that the patient trusted her physician—but later Breuer admitted to Freud the disturbing observation that toward the end of the treatment the patient expressed erotically tinged feelings toward her doctor. These reactions (later termed *transference*) occurred with some regularity in other patients as well.

Freud and Breuer's initial theory was basically simple: An experience which is accompanied by a strong emotion (affect) is usually overcome when the emotion is adequately expressed. A hysterical symptom, on the other hand, is formed when (for reasons which were not clearly spelled out at the time) the affect becomes strangulated. Barred from direct expression, the affect change finds a devious route, giving rise to a hysterical symptom. When under hypnosis the process is reversed, and the feeling is recalled and expressed, the symptom disappears. The process by which this feat is accomplished was called *abreaction,* and the cure was called *catharsis,* a draining off of emotional energies.

From these beginnings Freud developed a complex theory of psychological functioning, human development, and psychotherapy.

Basic Formulations

THE NEUROTIC CONFLICT

Freud's conceptions of psychotherapy, as they evolved over the years, cannot be understood without reference to his views concerning the nature of the patient's disturbance and its origins, which he traced to early childhood. The small child, according to Freud, is governed by powerful drives (subsumed under the headings of sexuality and aggression) which he must learn to control and channel along socially acceptable lines. The untrammeled expression of these strivings is curbed as a result of the parents' efforts to socialize the child. The child must learn to find a viable balance between the inner forces that propel him toward immediate gratification of his instinctual drives, part and parcel of his biological heritage, and the demands of external reality which demand delay of gratification and socially approved expression. Because of a basic incompatibility between these two goals, neurotic conflicts are an inevitable consequence of civilization, and emotional maturity is always a matter of degree. Neurotic disturbances (including the formation of symptoms) result from adverse childhood experiences which have prevented the growing organism from coming to terms with this dilemma, from an inordinate strength of his instinctual strivings, or from a combination of these.

In the process of growing up, the child internalizes the demands of reality and develops a set of psychological mechanisms which permit him to mediate between his inner needs and reality as the parents reflect it. He develops an ego and a superego as well as a network of defenses which serve to control his inner strivings. While psychological conflict cannot be avoided, most people somehow come to terms with their inner strivings and adjust them to the external world. The neurotic patient, on the other hand, has failed to do so, and he continues a futile struggle to arrive at a satisfactory compromise. The major symptom of a neurotic conflict, and a clue to its presence, is the affect of anxiety. Anxiety, according to Freud, signifies inadequate control over instinctual strivings and the existence of faulty defenses.

The task of psychotherapy is to help the patient resolve the difficulty, and this goal is accomplished by strengthening his ego, that is, by increasing his control over his inner needs, which the patient typically hides from himself.

TRANSFERENCE

The concept of the transference is the pivot upon which psychoanalytic therapy turns.

As we have seen, Freud and Breuer observed that patients in the course of hypnotic treatment developed emotional attachments to their therapist, which at the time seemed to be a most unwelcome complication. Subsequently, Freud, working alone, realized that the strong feelings which the patient was developing toward the therapist could not be explained on the basis of their *current* interaction. Eventually, he concluded that it was this very tendency to experience toward persons in the patient's current life, and especially toward the therapist, feelings that intrinsically had nothing to do with these persons which constituted the core of the illness. While initially the observations dealt primarily with erotic, positive feelings, Freud soon noted that when these feelings were not reciprocated by the therapist, they had a tendency to turn into the opposite. Thus, the therapist became the recipient of hostile, angry, hateful feelings, which, realistically, made as little sense as the earlier, positive ones.

Essentially, *transference* refers to this tendency to transfer to contemporaries strong feelings that at one time the patient experienced toward significant figures of his childhood, notably his parents. While Freud regarded transference as a universal phenomenon, it is particularly pronounced in neurotic patients. It emerges with powerful force when the therapist assumes a relatively passive, neutral, and shadowy role vis-à-vis the patient and when he encourages him to report unreservedly and honestly his train of thought (free association), with emphasis on dreams, fantasies, and reveries. The patient unwittingly recreates with the therapist the very conflict he had failed to resolve in relation to the parents of his childhood as the principal representatives of external reality; thus the therapeutic situation facilitates a relieving of earlier struggles. Stated otherwise, the neurotic patient suffers from what once had been an interpersonal conflict which he internalized and which has become an intrapsychic one. The therapeutic situation reverses the process and transforms the patient's intrapsychic conflict once again into an interpersonal one. Through this process psychoanalytic psychotherapy attempts to help the patient achieve a new and more adaptive solution.

The point that psychoanalytic therapy deals with conflictual material *as it occurs in the present* deserves special emphasis because it is frequently misunderstood by critics who accuse analytic psychotherapists of excessive preoccupation with the past. Furthermore, it must be underscored that the core of analytic therapy consists of the reliving of a conflict in the context of strong *affect in the present*.

THE TASK OF PSYCHOTHERAPY

As we have seen, the neurotic, according to Freud, suffers from an intrapsychic conflict which has its roots in early childhood but which is still a potent force in the patient's adult life, as evidenced by such symptoms as anxiety, depression, compulsions, obsessions, and phobias. The therapeutic situation is designed to bring such conflicts into the open. This task is accomplished by asking the patient to assume a relaxed position and to report to the therapist whatever thoughts and feelings arise in his awareness. In principle, this sounds like an easy assignment; in practice it turns out to be extraordinarily difficult. The difficulties are twofold:

1. The patient will soon encounter ideas and feelings which he does not wish to share with the therapist, and which he will consciously suppress.

2. Despite a strong desire to cooperate with the therapist, the patient finds that at times he becomes silent, "blocks," dwells on details, reports that "nothing occurs to me," etc.

These difficulties are called *resistance;* and, as might be expected, the former are more readily dealt with than the latter. Resistances of the second kind are seen as the result of unconscious defensive operations over which the patient has no control but which serve the function of excluding unpleasant and painful affect from awareness. The therapist's primary task is to help the patient overcome these resistances, an undertaking which is aided principally by interpretations. *Interpretations* are communications designed (1) to identify the presence of resistances, (2) to call them to the patient's attention, and (3) to advance reasonable hypotheses concerning the reasons for their existence. Another function of interpretations is to help the patient understand the nature of his conflict, which however cannot be done until the resistances are overcome. In practice these kinds of interpretations are often difficult to differentiate, but by far the larger part of the therapeutic effort consists in overcoming the patient's resistances. Through this process the patient gains increased ego control, and he grows in strength and independence. At the same time, interpretations lessen the patient's transference involvement with the therapist. Therapy terminates when the patient has achieved greater ego control, his symptoms have decreased, and significant aspects of the transference have been clarified.

This process, called *working through,* typically requires long periods of time (not rarely several years), and it is tedious, painful, and expensive both in terms of money and the participants' emotional expenditure.

Why is the process of psychoanalytic therapy so protracted and cumbersome? Prominent reasons include:

1. Despite a conscious desire to change and to achieve relief from his suffering, the neurotic patient (like everyone else) is unwittingly committed to the maintenance of the status quo. Change inevitably means the experiencing of very painful affects, and the patient, like an injured animal which reflexly shirks and even fights helpful ministrations, resists the efforts of the therapist as soon as a sensitive area is encountered. Thus, the therapist must realize that he is always dealing with a patient who is divided against himself and whose desire to cooperate cannot always be relied upon. Basic to this realization is Freud's conception of strong psychic forces which operate outside of awareness but which powerfully influence the feelings, attitudes, and actions of everyone.

2. While the neurotic patient's "solution" to his conflicts is maladaptive and self-defeating, nevertheless, it is one way of dealing with his problems, and it is the only one he knows and is able to entertain. Moreover, psychoanalytic therapists realize that they are dealing with personality and behavior patterns that are deeply ingrained and which have been repeated and reinforced throughout the person's life. These patterns have been acquired in childhood when the person was bio-

logically and psychologically dependent upon nurturing adults, and this state of great malleability cannot be easily reinstated. The task of therapy is almost comparable to inducing a person to unlearn the multiplication table or his mother tongue. However, not only must he unlearn faulty patterns, he must also acquire new ones, which may be likened to the acquisition of a complex skill, like playing the piano or learning a foreign language. These tasks, while not impossible, are extraordinarily difficult, particularly if the learner, for reasons he only dimly comprehends, fights every step of the way. The weapons he uses constitute the gamut of neurotic mechanisms, such as negativism, spite, domination, helplessness, hostility, anger, despair, etc., and they are the same ones he used in childhood to fight his parents in their efforts to socialize him. The therapist must learn to communicate with the unhappy, frustrated, and rebellious child within the adult patient, and at the same time enlist the adult and reasonable aspects of the patient's personality in the struggle. This requires a great amount of empathy, respect, patience, and understanding. Consequently, psychoanalysis can never be short, and therapeutic learning is always painful.

3. The psychoanalytic therapist, at least in principle, subscribes to the view of encouraging the patient to find his own answers to his problems in living. He confronts the patient with his inner contradictions and inconsistencies as they emerge in the course of therapy; he exposes his conflicts but he does not offer prescriptions for dealing with them. He may outline alternatives but in the end the patient, as an adult, must lead his own life and assume responsibility for his feelings and actions as well as their consequences. The process of therapy in some sense may be regarded as a process of weaning the patient from dependency (as mirrored by transference feelings) and inducing him, partly against his desire, to stand on his own feet. The therapist also feels that he can best accomplish this objective when from the beginning of therapy he treats the patient as an adult. His stance, from an external perspective, is therefore often seen as one of insufficient caring and even callousness. While being empathic and respectful, he avoids pampering the patient, and he does not spare him growing pains, disappointments, and at times disillusionment at the fact that a child's expectations of the world cannot be achieved by an adult except at great personal loss of integrity and self-respect. These

lessons are hard. They involve a good deal of trial and error, false starts, and backsliding. However, if independence, autonomy and self-direction are worthy goals, the therapist must let the patient struggle. Here, as elsewhere, some people learn faster than others, but it is hard to conceive that important lessons affecting one's life style can be learned in short order.

Other Pioneers

As Freud's work attracted increasing attention, he acquired a circle of disciples, some of whom disagreed with his theoretical views, and in a number of instances these theoretical divergences also produced modifications in the techniques. Freud himself maintained that any form of psychotherapy which accepts the basic concepts of transference, resistance, and the existence of unconscious processes has a right to call itself psychoanalysis. Important names in the history of psychoanalysis, which can be mentioned only in passing, include: Carl G. Jung, Alfred Adler, Otto Rank, Karl Abraham, Sandor Ferenczi, Paul Federn, Wilhelm Reich, Melanie Klein, Siegfried Bernfeld, Heinz Hartmann, Otto Fenichel, and Anna Freud. Their contributions deepened and extended Freud's insights.

NEO-FREUDIANS

Another group of workers, likewise important contributors to psychoanalytic theory and practice, consists of individuals who placed increasing emphasis on socioenvironmental and cultural factors which they felt had been insufficiently stressed by Freud in discussion of the genesis of neurotic disturbances. They took particular issue with Freud's biological orientation and his emphasis on instinctual drives, rejecting those aspects of his theory. They also studied in greater detail man's adaptive functions and constructive forces in his efforts to achieve competence, mastery, and identity (ego psychology). With regard to therapeutic practice, they introduced modifications, some of which have remained controversial. In general, it may be said that despite different terminology and new departures they built on Freud's foundation. The rise of the fascist movement in Germany prior to World War II, with its predictable antipathy toward psycho-analysis, caused a large-scale exodus of its adherents, most of whom emigrated to the United States, which provided a hospitable climate, particularly in the large urban centers. Members of this group, which also comprises some native Americans, include: Erich Fromm, Karen Horney, Franz Alexander, Frieda Fromm-Reichmann, Harry Stack Sullivan, Clara Thompson, and Erik H. Erikson.

Critical Assessments

ADVANTAGES

In view of the writer's admitted bias in favor of psychoanalytic psy-chotherapy, its positive features are implicit in the preceding discus-sion. In general it may be said that psychoanalytic psychotherapy rep-resents modern man's most ambitious attempt to deal with neurotic problems. It is a radical form of psychotherapy in the sense of at-tempting changes in the patient's total life-style within which neurotic symptoms are embedded. It is in principle opposed to the goal of modifying the patient's behavior by coercion or other forms of psycho-logical influence and instead focuses on the task of increasing the pa-tient's efforts toward independence, autonomy, and self-direction. Its major appeal is to reason and rational self-control, and it proceeds on the working assumption that the patient's emotional understanding of the forces that motivate him permits their control. Its respect for the individual and his right for self-determination is unequaled (with the possible exception of client-centered therapy—see Chapter 3). Finally, it offers a set of rational techniques toward these objectives.

CRITICISMS

In order to deal with the shortcomings of psychoanalysis as a form of psychotherapy, it is necessary to differentiate it from the psychoanaly-tic theory of personality and personality development, with which we are not here concerned. At the same time, the psychoanalytic theory of psychotherapy, as we have seen, shades into the personality theory, particularly in terms of its conceptions regarding neurotic conflicts and their genesis. However, the actual operations of psychotherapy—and this judgment applies to all contemporary theories—are not nearly as closely articulated to the theoretical substrate as the proponents would have one believe. Thus, there is a considerable hiatus between the therapist's actual interventions (including the therapist's intent) and the theoretical framework to which he subscribes. Consequently, it is possible that the actual operations of psychotherapy can be more adequately explained in terms of concepts other than those espoused by Freud and his followers. Indeed, it is this writer's belief that the psychoanalytic theory of therapy (in addition to the personality theory) is in need of a major overhaul to bring it in line with advances in psychology, sociology, anthropology, and biology.

Implied in the preceding account is a distinction between what therapists *do* and *what they say they do*. Criticisms of psychoanalytic therapy are frequently directed at the practices of individual therapists, whose competence undoubtedly varies as much as that of other professionals. In as complex a field as psychotherapy, where patient, therapist, and situational variables interact in exceedingly intricate ways, it is hardly surprising that circumstances frequently conspire to make the therapeutic enterprise less than ideal. As is true in education, medicine, and any other human activity, the best efforts often fail. To criticize psychoanalytic therapy on those grounds seems less than fair.

Specific problems pertaining to the assessment of therapeutic outcomes will be considered elsewhere in this volume. While precise data are hard to come by, numerous studies suggest that psychoanalytic psychotherapy results in favorable changes in a fair percentage of the cases (perhaps in the vicinity of 50 to 60 percent).

With respect to the efficiency of this form of psychotherapy, there is no denying that it is tedious, painstaking, and time-consuming, hence expensive. Whether expectable returns in a given instance are commensurate with the investment of time, money, and energy is a delicate question, and it is a judgment involving considerations of the price tag one places on neurotic suffering and its contrasting states, maturity and autonomy.

The assertation that psychoanalytic psychotherapy holds promise only for certain kinds of patients (who possess a fairly high level of intelligence, youth, ability to take some distance from their problems and look at themselves objectively, motivation for change, perseverance in the face of adversity, and whose life situation is already characterized by a fair degree of independence and autonomy) undeniably has much truth in it. Also, there are some kinds of problems (the so-called transference neuroses) for which psychoanalytic therapy is more suitable. The fact that psychoanalysis is sometimes employed inappropriately may attest to a therapist's poor judgment, but predictions in this area are hazardous, and there are undoubtedly many instances in which a therapist may decide to work with a patient despite seemingly insuperable odds.

The fact that psychoanalytic therapy, because of its great cost, has largely been confined to members of the upper and upper middle classes is indisputable and reflects the inequities of our social system. While the number of patients who can be helped by psychoanalytic therapy will of necessity remain small relative to the widespread need for therapeutic services, there is no cogent reason for keeping it a luxury item. Just as higher education is now available to most qualified applicants irrespective of their financial resources, similar arrangements could be worked out for persons in need of analytic therapy. In this context, the exploitation and corruption of Freud's intellectual heritage—the bequest of an uncompromisingly honest man whose fight against hypocrisy and oppression rightfully marks him as one of mankind's great liberators—by professional guilds in the United States which have been more interested in the creation of exclusive "clubs" than the advancement of knowledge is an evil which has done serious, and perhaps irreversible, damage to the viability of psychoanalytic psychotherapy.

Suggested Readings

FENICHEL, O. *The psychoanalytical theory of neurosis.* New York: Norton, 1945.

FINE, R. *Freud: A critical re-evaluation of his theories.* New York: McKay, 1962.

FREUD, S. Complete psychological works of . . . J. Strachey (Ed.). London: Hogarth Press and the Institute of Psycho-Analysis, 1955–   . 24 vols.

FREUD, S. Collected papers of . . . A. & J. Strachey (Trans.). Hogarth Press and the Institute of Psycho-Analysis, 1950. 5 vols.

GREENSON, R. R. *The technique and practice of psychoanalysis.* Vol. I. New York: International Universities Press, 1967.

HENDRICK, I. *Facts and theories of psychoanalysis.* (3d rev. ed.) New York: Knopf, 1958.

HORNEY, K. *New ways in psychoanalysis.* New York: Norton, 1939.

MARMOR, J. (Ed.) *Modern psychoanalysis: New directions and perspectives.* (2d ed.) New York: Basic Books, 1968.

MENNINGER, K. *Theory of psychoanalytic technique.* New York: Basic Books, 1958.

MUNROE, R. L. *Schools of psychoanalytic thought.* New York: Dryden, 1955.

SULLIVAN, H. S. *The collected works of Harry Stack Sullivan.* New York: Basic Books, 1964. 2 vols.

ZILBOORG, G., & HENRY, G. W. *A history of medical psychology.* New York: Norton, 1941.

CHAPTER 3

CLIENT-CENTERED
PSYCHOTHERAPY

Background

Like other forms of psychotherapy, client-centered therapy is largely the creation of one man who succeeded in vigorously advancing his point of view and over a period of time attracted a sizeable following of students and adherents. Client-centered therapy (initially called nondirective therapy) is the brainchild of Carl R. Rogers (born 1902), a psychologist, who began formulating his ideas around 1938. The viewpoint underwent further development while Rogers was on the faculty of Ohio State University (1940 through 1945), reaching its culmination in the mid-1950s when Rogers headed the Counseling Center at the University of Chicago. One of Rogers' major works, *Client-centered Psychotherapy*, was published in 1950, and the appearance of a report on an extensive research project (Rogers & Dymond, 1954) deepened the acceptance of client-centered thinking in America. Though he originally designed it as a form of therapy applicable primarily to neurotic patients, Rogers became interested in exploring its potential with severely disturbed psychotic patients. Beginning around 1960, this work was carried out at the University of Wisconsin (Rogers, Gendlin, Kiesler, & Truax, 1967). In more recent years Rogers has become less interested in individual psychotherapy and has turned to work with groups composed of normal subjects who wish to increase their sensitivity to interpersonal experience and become more "open" in dealings with their peers. Concomitantly, Rogers left the academic setting, eventually starting an institute of his own in California. There are indications that client-centered therapy has lost some of its momentum in recent years, a development which may be due to the rise of behavior therapy as well as a decline in the vigorous leadership which Rogers exercised in earlier years.

Basic Formulations

THE PHENOMENOLOGICAL FRAMEWORK

Client-centered therapy from its inception has stressed the inner phenomenological world of the _client,_ a term chosen in preference to _patient,_ partly to underscore the value placed on the self-determination and autonomy of the individual, partly to highlight the difference between client-centered therapy and other forms of psychotherapy which grew out of medicine and psychiatry. Client-centered therapy is a uniquely psychological theory and therapy, which may account for its popularity among psychologists, social workers, marriage counselors, ministers of all faiths, child therapists, and others; it has won disciples in many other countries as well. Basically, it is an existentialist-humanistic approach but without the elaborate philosophical underpinnings characteristic of the psychotherapies based on the writings of Husserl, Heidegger, Sartre, Binswanger, and other Europeans. While influenced by the writings of Otto Rank, a student of Freud's, and American theorists like G. H. Mead and Harry Stack Sullivan, Rogers' work is largely his own creation. From its inception, client-centered therapy has rejected both the dynamic formulations of Freud and the views of the learning theorists (see Chapter 4 on Behavior Therapy).

Client-centered therapy focuses on the therapeutic relationship as the vehicle for personality change and places primary emphasis on the client's moment-to-moment experience in the therapeutic framework. The psychotherapeutic relationship is in principle indistinguishable from any good human relationship in which a person feels fully accepted, respected, and prized. The client, therefore, is not a patient who is sick and who is in need of treatment, but he is a person whose earlier experiences in life have made him defensive, severed him from free and open communication with his peers, and prevented him from realizing his potential as a fully functioning person.

This view of the client has numerous implications for diagnosis as well as treatment. Indeed, both terms are eschewed by client-centered therapists. For one thing, if the client is not viewed as a patient whose personality and behavior are seen in need of change (particularly by others, including the therapist), the problem of diagnosis becomes immaterial. Since the client-centered therapist avoids "evaluation" of all kinds, he is equally opposed to the diagnostic process in the course of which a professional person external to the client determines "objectively" what is "wrong" and formulates a treatment plan designed to correct a set of feelings, attitudes, or behaviors. Client-centered therapy, therefore, does not consist of techniques designed to produce specific changes, but it is a unified approach to interpersonal experience. Thus, client-centered therapy is applicable to all individuals regardless of the nature of their interpersonal disturbance, although it is probably more suitable to individuals who have already achieved a fair measure of maturity and integration. Particularly in the early years, client-centered therapy attracted primarily college students and other intelligent members of the middle class whose disturbances were relatively minor, and therapy was usually brief (often in the neighborhood of ten sessions). The short-term character of the therapy, however, is not a defining characteristic, and many clients have been seen over long periods of time.

Another implication is that the client is fully responsible for the conduct of his life. Respect for the client's autonomy and independence dictates the therapist's noninterference regardless of the exigencies of the situation. The changes which accrue to the client as a result of client-centered therapy are to a large extent changes in his inner world and in his self-concept. Client-centered therapy is not a form of behavior modification, and the therapist is not concerned with effecting any *specific* changes in the client's attitudes; he is even less preoccupied with effecting changes in overt behavior. The focus throughout rests on the client's experience, especially his "experiencing" (Gendlin, 1962) in the therapeutic relationship. Concomitantly, there is no interest in the client's past, the causes or antecedents of his difficulties, and the specifics of his current life situation which may contribute to his problems in living. Strictly speaking, the only thing that matters is what happens between client and therapist in the here and now of the therapeutic encounter.

THE THERAPIST

As we have seen, the client is not an organism to be treated, manipulated, or changed. Instead, he is a participant in a human relationship which enables him to explore his feelings and attitudes and which becomes therapeutic by virtue of a set of attitudes brought to bear by the therapist. In fact, the therapist's attitudes are the therapeutic force and the fulcrum which moves the client-centered therapeutic enterprise. These include prominently: (1) the therapist's genuineness, or congruence; (2) the therapist's acceptance, or unconditional positive regard for his client; and (3) the therapist's accurate and empathic understanding of the client. Rogers (1957) has termed the therapist's attitudes "the necessary and sufficient" conditions for constructive personality change.

Genuineness of the therapist. This attitude, considered by Rogers the most basic ingredient of therapeutic success, is characterized by the therapist's openness to another person's experience and a keen awareness of himself and the client's experience. The therapist is himself and he is without pretense; he meets the client on a person-to-person basis, which in turn permits the reflection of feelings communicated to the therapist by the patient. In the early stages of client-centered therapy, reflections of feeling were regarded as the principal "technique" employed by the therapist, but with the declining emphasis upon technology, the essence of the therapist's genuineness is now viewed as an attitude which is communicated to the client both verbally and nonverbally.

Rogers points out that this attitude does not imply that the therapist will burden the client with his personal feelings or will overtly express all his feelings. He does not present a professional facade or hide strong and persistent feelings from himself and his client. In short, he must be open to his own experience as well as that of his client, and he must be able to communicate this openness to the client. Thus there eventuates a direct personal encounter between two human beings which is devoid of sham or duplicity, and it is this encounter which permits the client to be himself. Rogers asserts that when the therapist is genuine in the relationship he creates the most important condition for effective psychotherapy. The remaining two sets of attitudes, while important, are seen as less crucial.

Unconditional positive regard. The second aspect of the therapist's attitude consists of an unqualified acceptance of the client as a person to be prized. It means that the therapist refrains from evaluations or moral judgments of the client's feelings or conduct; thus he creates a condition which permits the client to feel secure, protected, respected, and fully accepted. As this attitude is communicated to the client both on a verbal and nonverbal level, he begins to explore his feelings and shares his experiences with the therapist as a representative of reality who can be trusted and who respects the client's confidence. The importance of this attitude can hardly be overestimated, and while other forms of psychotherapy have advocated a similar attitude on the part of the therapist, client-centered therapy has been more explicit about its constructive influence. Stated otherwise, whereas psychoanalytic therapy, for example, regards the therapist's attitude of respect and acceptance as a precondition for the technical interventions (interpretations), client-centered therapy has elevated unconditional positive regard to the status of a powerful therapeutic force in its own right.

It may be seen that this attitude represents a radical departure from what the client has learned to expect from significant persons in his life, who have often criticized, disapproved, demeaned, and castigated him not only for his actions but also for his fantasies, wishes, and impulses. Moreover, because the client has internalized these attitudes, he has become his own most severe critic and has come to feel guilty. Therefore, the suspiciousness, guilt, and secrecy which are characteristic of the neurotic patient and constitute his defenses against further injury to his self-esteem are met with a diametrically opposed attitude whose effect is to instill in the client a growing sense of trust.

The adjective "unconditional" serves to emphasize the requirement that the therapist attach no conditions to his acceptance. Instead, the therapist's acceptance encompasses equally "good" and "bad" feelings; indeed, he accepts *all* the client's feelings as integral parts of the personality. The therapist's unconditional positive regard extends to feelings commonly termed hostile, destructive, vengeful, greedy, and many others—all disapproved by society as well as the client. In brief, the client comes to feel that the therapist really cares.

Accurate empathy. Finally, the therapist must be able to feel thoroughly in tune with the client's moment-to-moment experience; that is, he must be at home in the client's inner world. The therapist must reverberate to the client's feelings and recognize the presence of feelings even when they are poorly articulated by the client. This sensitivity implies that the therapist must be familiar with the spectrum of human emotions and that he must be able to experience the identical feelings the client is currently experiencing, albeit without reacting to them by rejection or hostility and without getting lost in the client's phenomenal world. For example, if the client is experiencing anger, the therapist must sense the presence of this affect and communicate this understanding to the client. However, accurate empathy prevents him from judging these feelings or from feeling personally threatened by them. Again, it should be emphasized that empathy is considered a prime qualification for the psychotherapist in other forms of psychotherapy as well, although it is typically regarded as a precondition for personality change rather than as a therapeutic force.

THE THERAPEUTIC PROCESS

Rogers describes the essence of the therapeutic process in client-centered therapy as follows:

> In a broad sense the process may be described as the client's reciprocation of the therapist's attitudes. As he finds someone listening to him with consistent acceptance while he expresses his thoughts and feelings, the client, little by little, becomes increasingly able to listen to communications from within himself; he becomes able to realize that he is angry, or that he *is* frightened, or that he *is* experiencing feelings of love. Gradually, he becomes able to listen to feelings within himself which have previously seemed so bizarre, so terrible, or so disorganizing that they have been shut off completely from conscious awareness. As he reveals these hidden and "awful" aspects of himself, he finds that the therapist's regard for him remains unshaken. And, slowly, he moves toward adopting the same attitude toward himself, toward accepting himself as he is, and thus prepares to move forward in the process of becoming. Finally, as the client is able to listen to more of himself, he moves toward greater congruence, toward expressing all of himself more openly. He is, at last, free to change and grow in the directions which are natural to the human organism [1967, p. 1226].

It may be seen that the therapist's attitudes, outlined above, initiate a process within the client which causes him to move from defensiveness to openness, from oppression to freedom of expression, from being frozen to becoming alive, from stagnation to growth, from immaturity to maturity, from self-centeredness to selfhood. He begins to experience, often for the first time, his own feelings and is not ashamed to accept them as his own. There occurs a general loosening up, accompanied by a greater readiness to relate to others and to share his experiences with them. The neurotic rigidity disappears and gives way to a greater capacity for living in the present.

Emphasis on Research

Almost from its inception, client-centered therapy has welcomed and indeed embraced open inquiry into the therapeutic process. In this important sense, client-centered therapy has taken its place and remained within the mainstream of academic psychology, and the psychological profession has recognized Rogers' significant contributions through numerous awards and by electing him president of the American Psychological Association.

Rogers' emphasis on the study of empirical data led him to pioneer sound recordings of actual therapeutic interviews, an innovation which required considerable courage in the 1940s, when the privacy of the therapist's chamber was considered inviolable. Subsequently, Rogers produced sound films and encouraged his students to maintain careful records of the therapeutic transaction. These innovations were brought about by the belief that it is more important to examine the empirical data of psychotherapy than the theoretical statements, and that psychotherapy must be studied like any other psychological process. The impetus given to research by client-centered therapy is at least equal in importance to Rogers' theoretical contributions or the effectiveness of his form of psychotherapy. Certainly, in the 1940s and 1950s the bulk of the research publications in psychotherapy came from within the client-centered school. In the 1960s the publications of behavior therapists have eclipsed the number of research studies contributed by client-centered therapists although probably not their importance.

A major focus of research on client-centered therapy, as in other forms of psychotherapy, has been on the question of effectiveness. Through a number of studies investigators demonstrated that clients experience significant changes in feelings and attitudes, and perhaps to a lesser extent in behavior. There is evidence to show that clients become more integrated (as shown for example, through self-descriptions obtained from a set of cards, technically called a Q-sort, as well as projective tests), less neurotic, more open to experience, more real-istic, more accepting of themselves and others, more capable of with-standing frustration, less defensive, and better able to cope with prob-lems in living. While treated groups of clients in general showed greater improvements than untreated controls, it cannot be asserted that the research has adduced unequivocal evidence that link the changes specifically to the therapeutic conditions created by the ther-apist. Furthermore, the fact that other forms of therapy claim changes very similar to those reported by client-centered therapists invites the speculation that common factors in all forms of psychotherapy, which may also be present in client-centered therapy, may be responsible for the effects. At any rate, the evidence is clear that changes do occur, and frequently they are measurable after a relatively short course of treatment. To this must be added, however, that the results are more impressive for relatively mild disturbances than for seriously disturbed psychotic patients.

Beyond the measurement of therapeutic outcomes, client-centered therapy has contributed a wealth of studies dealing with the process of therapy, that is, the moment-to-moment client-therapist interaction. Examples of such studies are: therapist responses to particular kinds of patient communications; content analyses of verbal interchanges between the participants; comparisons between the communications of experienced and inexperienced therapists; the patient's verbaliza-tions in the course of initial interviews as a predictor of therapeutic change, and many others. The following study is a representative ex-ample:

A typical study. Shlien, Mosak, and Dreikurs (1960) investigated the effects of time limits upon outcome. To measure improvement, they computed coefficients of correlation between descriptions of the client as he saw himself and as he would like to be (self versus ideal self). It had been found earlier that in disturbed clients there is a marked discrepancy between descriptions of the real self and the ideal self; conversely, as the client improves, the congruence between self and ideal self increases, reflected by a rise in the correlation coeffi-cient. Five groups were used in this study: (1) a control group of pa-tients who applied for therapy, who were tested, and asked to wait for three months before therapy started; (2) a control group of normal

Fig. 3-1 *Mean correlation chart. Changes in coefficients of correlation between real self and ideal self in therapy and control groups. [From Shlien, Mosak, & Dreikurs (1960).]*

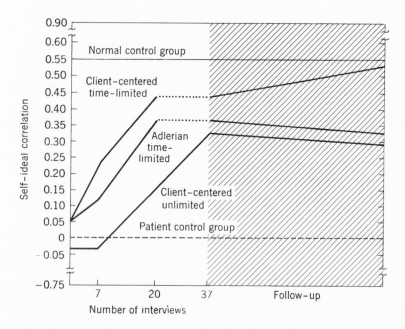

subjects; (3) a group of thirty patients who applied for client-centered therapy and who were free to begin and end therapy when they wished (mean of thirty-seven interviews); (4) a group of twenty patients who were offered therapy under time-limited conditions (maximum of twenty interviews, twice a week); (5) a group of patients (number unreported) seen by Adlerian therapists in a different setting, under the same time-limited conditions as Group (4). Figure 3-1 represents the results in terms of mean self-ideal correlations obtained at preselected intervals.

It is seen that the passage of time had no effect on the normal and patient control groups as far as mean self-ideal correlations were concerned. Second, all therapy groups showed marked improvement, particularly between the seventh and twentieth interviews. Gains were maintained on follow-up. Finally, the two time-limited groups improved more rapidly than the unlimited group, although the level at termination was about the same. The authors concluded that time-limited therapy was not only as effective as unlimited therapy, but it was also twice as efficient since roughly identical results were achieved in half the number of interviews. Although precise data were not reported, the therapists were apparently more experienced than is often true for research studies in which trainees are used because of their ready availability as subjects. In interpreting the results, we must also keep in mind that they are entirely based on self-reports, and no evidence is presented on changes in observable behavior.

Research in psychotherapy typically does not lead to new discoveries nor does it give rise to changes in technique, the selection of clients, or theoretical convictions. Research always serves a confirmatory function, and in client-centered therapy it has indeed supported Rogers' formulations. Nevertheless, it must be reiterated that so-called crucial experiments are not possible in psychotherapy (or, for that matter, in other areas of psychology), so that one can never prove that one's theoretical assumptions are the only, or the best ones, to account for the changes that are observed. It is entirely possible that different assumptions may account equally well for the data. On the other hand, empirical research is essential if the field is to advance beyond clinical observations. The client-centered school has faced up to this responsibility.

Critical Assessment

ADVANTAGES

The client-centered formulations as well as their actual operations are quite parsimonious, easily understood, and readily communicated. Its theoretical superstructure is relatively simple, and the theoretical assumptions are closely linked to the therapeutic strategies. It is perhaps this immediate appeal that accounts more than any other factor for the wide acceptance and popularity of Rogers' theories. The therapeutic conditions, described by Rogers, of course represent an ideal which no one can continuously live up to in practice. However, the basic ingredients of therapeutic practice can be taught fairly readily, and the principles make greater demands on innate capacities of the young therapist than on formal training.

CRITICISMS

The system appears to be open to a number of criticisms, among which the following are salient:

1. Client-centered therapy shows a cavalier disregard for the problem of *diagnosis.* It is undeniable that prospective patients suffer from a wide variety of psychological disorders ranging from mild disturbances to severe problems in living. Often there are psychosomatic symptoms which require both psychotherapy and medical management; in the case of schizophrenia, in addition to the psychological aspects of the disorder, there may be biochemical imbalances and genetic factors which complicate the situation. In short, the patient's genetic and constitutional makeup as well as his life history are important determinants of his current difficulties, and all may play an important part in arriving at a meaningful prognosis. To assert, as client-centered therapists do, that diagnosis is evaluative and judgmental is a half-truth which is contradicted by the foregoing considerations. To be sure, diagnostic procedures often serve to pin a label on a patient which may at the same time communicate society's censure of deviant behavior. However, the above factors must be weighed before accepting a patient for psychotherapy. Furthermore, if the therapist's training does not include broad clinical experience—and client-centered therapy in keeping with its theoretical position contends that such training is unnecessary and perhaps even undesirable—neither is he equipped to make a realistic assessment of the patient's current difficulties nor can he assess the possible degree of success of his therapeutic approach. If the client-centered therapist attempts to solve the problem by referring the prospective client for diagnostic assessment to another professional, he is acting rationally, but this solution is inconsistent with the theory's basic assertion that diagnosis is superfluous.

2. Closely related to the preceding point is the argument that it is impossible for the therapist to be completely nonjudgmental or achieve unconditional positive regard. There is evidence to show that therapists like some patients better than others, and while the compe-

tent therapist should certainly endeavor to spare the client his personal opinions and value judgments, he cannot be the paragon of virtue client-centered therapy expects him to be. Genuineness and unconditional positive regard are at best ideals which may be approximated, but their full realization in a fallible world seems to be impossible.

3. As indicated in paragraph 1, client-centered therapy largely ignores psychopathology and clinical as well as experimental findings supporting this body of knowledge. The system similarly rejects the contributions of dynamic psychology (including such key concepts as transference and resistance, which Rogers dismisses as unfortunate consequences attributable to mishandling of the therapeutic relationship) as well as the learning theorist's contention that neurotic behaviors are learned and maintained by the patient's social environment. In fact, client-centered therapy largely ignores the work of other theorists and the advances that have been made by other behavioral sciences. Stated in another way, the client's view of himself and the world, while undeniably possessing a reality of its own, cannot be accepted at face value, and the therapist, as a professional, cannot escape being an external observer. As such, he must evaluate, judge, and at times oppose the client's phenomenal world. The client, by definition, distorts aspects of himself and the outer world. How can the therapist, simply by being genuine and by empathizing with the client's feelings, correct these distortions?

4. Client-centered therapy denies that the therapist's task is to *influence* the client and questions the relevance of *techniques* for personality change. If psychotherapy is not a set of techniques for influencing another person, it is patently futile to train psychotherapists. On the other hand, if it is admitted that therapists can be trained to acquire genuineness, unconditional positive regard, and empathy, the training itself will rob them of the spontaneity and genuineness which Rogers posits as the necessary and sufficient conditions for constructive personality change. It is quite likely that the therapist's attitudes are necessary conditions for therapeutic success, but it may be questioned whether they are sufficient for *maximal* change. In other words, a therapist possessing these attributes may be effective, but he might be more effective if he proceeded planfully in helping the client overcome obstacles, like phobic avoidance and strivings for depend-

ency. Rogers seems to assert that a good human relationship, characterized by acceptance and love, overcomes all problems in living, or that love is enough. Like all universal principles, this assertion is open to serious challenge.

In conclusion, client-centered therapy is more adequate as an *approach* to viewing persons who suffer from problems in living than as a set of *techniques* for effecting personality and behavior change. Its emphasis on the worth of the individual in an age which obscures this value is altogether wholesome and desirable. On the debit side, its utility is confined to a limited segment of clients who are relatively well-functioning individuals and who have the personality resources which permit them to profit from the kind of experience client-centered therapy can provide. As a therapeutic technology it has severe limitations, and its very tenets preclude the possibility of sharpening and extending the system as a therapeutic force.

Suggested Readings

ALLPORT, G. *Becoming*. New Haven, Conn.: Yale, 1955.

BUBER, M. *The knowledge of man*. New York: Harper & Row, 1965.

ROGERS, C. R. *Client-centered therapy*. Boston: Houghton Mifflin, 1951.

ROGERS, C. R. *On becoming a person*. Boston: Houghton Mifflin, 1961.

ROGERS, C. R. Persons or science? A philosophical question. *American Psychologist*, 1955, **10**, 267–278.

ROGERS, C. R. The necessary and sufficient conditions of therapeutic personality change. *Journal of Consulting Psychology*, 1957, **21**, 95–103.

ROGERS, C. R. Toward a science of the person. In T. W. Wann (Ed.), *Behaviorism and phenomenology*. Chicago: University of Chicago, 1964. Pp. 109–133.

ROGERS, C. R., & DYMOND, R. F. (Eds.) *Psychotherapy and personality change*. Chicago: University of Chicago, 1954.

CHAPTER 4

BEHAVIOR THERAPY

ehavior therapy represents one of the newer approaches to the correction of disturbed or abnormal psychological functioning. It achieved considerable prominence during the last two decades, particularly in the United States and Great Britain. For reasons which will become apparent, it has considerable appeal to psychologists reared in the academic tradition, although a number of psychiatrists have played an important part in its development and have come to recognize its utility.

Criticisms of the Dynamic Approach

In an important sense the development of behavior therapy may be viewed as a powerful reaction against psychoanalysis and other "dynamic" therapies, which have been labeled by behavior therapists as "traditional." The disenchantment with psychoanalysis as a theory and technique for effecting therapeutic change may be summarized as follows:

1. Psychoanalysis (and other forms of dynamic therapies) have failed to demonstrate their therapeutic effectiveness. Eysenck, a British psychologist, has been a particularly vocal proponent of this position. In 1952 Eysenck compiled a number of studies dealing with treatment outcomes from which he concluded that psychoanalysis (as well as other "eclectic" forms of psychotherapy) produce results which are unimpressive and in no way superior to no treatment at all. While admitting numerous methodological difficulties in the published studies and in the comparisons he carried out, Eysenck asserted that in the absence of strong positive evidence it is legitimate to infer that traditional psychotherapy is largely ineffective and wasteful. Indeed, he went so far as to counsel against training more psychotherapists. In subsequent years Eysenck became convinced of the advantages of behavior therapy as an alternate therapeutic method and joined the camp of the behavior therapists as an ardent champion.

2. The psychoanalytic conceptions of neurosis are based on the "medical disease" model which is theoretically inadequate. Freud viewed all forms of behavior as determined by multiple causes and placed great emphasis on intrapsychic factors. A neurotic symptom, according to Freud, represents a compromise between incompatible

psychic forces. The psychoanalyst, therefore, is always concerned with underlying causes, and a neurotic symptom to him is a manifestation of a central neurotic process. A neurotic symptom, like the symptom fever, can have a variety of causes. Behavior therapists find this formulation unacceptable. They regard the symptom as the problem which needs to be dealt with. Their therapeutic focus thus rests on behavior rather than its antecedents, and it is behavior they seek to modify. Hence they prefer the term *behavior modification* to *psychotherapy*. They consider Freudian principles as insufficiently supported by empirical evidence, incapable of verification because of their vagueness, and lacking in practical utility.

3. The criticism pertaining to the absence of acceptable empirical evidence for the effectiveness of the dynamic therapies derives support from these additional considerations: (a) psychoanalysis and its variants are time-consuming, excessively expensive, and tedious; (b) they are applicable only to highly intelligent, educated, well-motivated, and affluent members of the upper middle class; (c) while their scope has been widened over the years, these methods are basically applicable only to the so-called transference neuroses (hysteria, obsessive-compulsive neurosis, and phobia) and are of minimal utility for a wide range of behavior disorders in which anxiety and personal discomfort are not distinguishing features. Accordingly, psychoanalysis has little to offer to the vast majority of patients seeking help, and alternative methods must be found which are more efficient, less costly, and less demanding of professional manpower.

It is easily seen that in a society which is becoming increasingly concerned with the welfare of all its citizens, an approach to psychotherapy which promises significant returns for relatively modest investments readily commands attention. What are the theoretical assumptions of behavior therapy and the techniques which are designed to supplant the older, more cumbersome methods?

While behavior therapists do not share a single theoretical approach or espouse a single set of therapeutic techniques, they are united in their emphasis on observable behavior. They regard all behavior, including neurotic and psychotic behavior, as learned and governed by the same principles which learning theorists have attempted to elucidate since the end of the nineteenth century. Basically, then, they are behaviorists in the tradition of Watson, but they also draw heavily on the theories of Pavlov, Thorndike, Hull, and Skinner. Their preference for one or the other theories determines variations in their conceptions of neurosis as well as their therapeutic techniques. Unlike the psychoanalysts, who trace their beginnings to clinical psychiatry and medicine, the behavior therapists have looked to the psychological laboratory and controlled experimentation as the model for their approach. While the relationship between laboratory research, particularly that involving animal studies, and clinical practice is by no means clear-cut, behavior therapists continually stress the need for controlled research and empirical verification.

According to the behavior therapists, disordered or neurotic behavior is not intrinsically different from so-called normal behavior except that it is considered maladaptive by the individual or by others, a judgment which also applies to psychotic behavior. Fundamentally, the therapist is dealing with faulty habits which have been learned through particular events in the person's life. Reinforcement has led from what initially may have been a fortuitous response to a troublesome situation. The antecedents are of no intrinsic interest to the behavior therapist except insofar as certain conditions which reward the person's neurotic behavior may still be present in his life. Neurotic or psychotic habits are formed in the same manner as any other habit and are sustained by the same conditions. In order to change such habits it is necessary to modify the consequences the behavior has for the individual. A child suffering from a school phobia, for example, may earn certain rewards by his avoidance of going to school. As long as there are positive results (or as long as he avoids negative ones), the behavior will be maintained. The treatment of disordered behavior, therefore, requires the modification of those conditions which serve to maintain it. The behavior therapist specifically rejects dynamic notions of central mechanisms or causes. To quote Eysenck:

> Learning theory does not postulate any "such unconscious causes," but regards neurotic symptoms as simple learned habits; there is no neurosis underlying the symptom, but merely the symptom itself. *Get rid of the symptom and you have eliminated the neurosis* [1959, p. 65].

Two Forms of Behavior Therapy

Contemporary behavior therapists fall into two major groups, (1) those following the classical or respondent learning theory of Pavlov, and (2) those adhering to the operant conditioning model of Skinner. The former approach, spearheaded by the American (formerly South African) psychiatrist Wolpe, has been applied prominently to the treatment of phobias, inhibitions, and sexual disorders in adults; the latter has been successfully employed with hospitalized psychotic patients, and children (including those with serious disturbances, such as autism). Both theories are stimulus-response theories, although Pavlov is more concerned with involuntary (autonomic) responses of the organism, whereas Skinner's focus rests upon the voluntary musculature (operant behavior). Major distinctions between the two theories are briefly characterized in the following pages.

THE WOLPEAN APPROACH

According to Pavlov, an originally innocuous stimulus which does not have the power to elicit a particular response may, through essentially fortuitous circumstances, become associated with a stimulus which does evoke a given response. The simultaneous occurrence and repetition of such stimuli lead to the formation of a conditioned response which is maintained and strengthened through reinforcement. Conditioned stimuli have the tendency to become generalized. Thus a child who experiences anxiety (an autonomic response) in the presence of a dog will generalize this response to other dogs and perhaps other four-legged animals, and he will avoid all situations which even remotely resemble the original anxiety-provoking situation. Thus a phobia may be formed. Accordingly, to unlearn a phobia it is necessary to reinstate the original anxiety situation (or a reasonable facsimile thereof) and to evoke a different response, preferably an antagonistic one. In this way the anxiety response will become inhibited and eventually extinguished. We shall see in greater detail how this technique is employed in clinical situations.

In contrast to Pavlov's emphasis upon respondent behavior, the thrust of Skinner's theory concerns voluntary (operant) behavior, which is mediated through the voluntary musculature. According to Skinner, from an early age the individual learns to "operate" upon the environment, and it is these responses which become part of his behavior repertoire when they are reinforced by persons in the environment. Reinforcement may occur through positive consequences, avoidance of negative ones, attention, etc. It can be shown, for example, that a child's autistic behavior—and the same applies to other forms of behavior—is maintained because the parents, perhaps unwittingly, reinforce it. The behavior therapist following Skinner's approach, therefore, is intent upon reinforcing those forms of behavior which he considers desirable, and he attempts to extinguish those he is intent upon eliminating. In this way behavior is gradually "shaped."

For present purposes it is sufficient to note that the respondent model pays greater attention to the manner in which stimulus and response become paired, whereas the operant approach is more concerned with the consequences of the individual's behavior. Differences in therapeutic technique, it will be noted, follow from these theoretical assumptions. A wide variety of techniques have been developed, all of which share the common characteristic of being aimed chiefly at the modification of overt behavior as opposed to the individual's inner state (feelings, attitudes, cognitions, etc.).

DESENSITIZATION AND COUNTERCONDITIONING TECHNIQUES

The techniques developed by Wolpe provide perhaps the best illustration of this form of behavior therapy. Originally applied primarily to the treatment of phobias, the technique has more recently been used in dealing with many other forms of disordered behavior.

In order to determine the nature of the problem, that is, the behavior to be modified and the techniques to be employed, Wolpe relies on a few fairly extensive interviews. If the patient, for example, presents as his problem a phobia of open places, Wolpe will attempt to determine specifically the kinds of situations or circumstances that evoke anxiety and the kinds of events which follow the occurrence of his fear. Usually it emerges that the patient experiences intense anxiety in specific situations, but there are others in which he reports milder forms of anxiety and discomfort. Using careful inquiry, the therapist in collaboration with the patient will construct a so-called anxiety hierarchy consisting of a graduated list of situations ranging from mild to extreme.

From the beginning of therapy, the patient receives systematic instruction in deep muscle relaxation, a technique originally developed by Jacobson and often combined with hypnosis. Subsequently, a portion of each therapy session is devoted to this procedure, which requires the patient to relax in a comfortable lounging chair. As therapy proceeds, he progressively learns to relax voluntary muscle groups in all parts of his body.

Once the patient has achieved a measure of mastery in this technique, the therapist asks him to imagine as vividly as possible scenes selected from the previously constructed anxiety hierarchy, starting at the low end. As soon as the patient experiences anxiety he is asked to signify this to the therapist, who will tell him to abandon the imagined scene and return to a relaxed position. This procedure is repeated until the patient is able to imagine situations increasingly higher in the hierarchy without experiencing anxiety. Eventually a point is reached at which the patient can imagine a situation previously experienced as highly anxiety-provoking without experiencing the original discomfort. When this juncture is reached, the patient has become desensitized to the phobia. If successful, the relaxation achieved in the therapeutic situation will generalize to the real-life situation, which is of course the purpose in all forms of psychotherapy.

Closely resembling the desensitization technique is the technique of *reciprocal inhibition,* and the two are frequently combined in practice. If a patient, for example, reacts to authority figures with timidity and submission (which may be the troublesome situation for which he seeks therapeutic help), the therapist will train him to make an antagonistic response incompatible with the maladaptive one. Sometimes patient and therapist will enact (role play) a typical scene. Wolpe has found that assertive and sexual responses are powerful antagonists to anxiety. Thus it is therapeutically effective to systematically condition the patient to oppose the maladaptive response with a stronger, more adaptive one. Desensitization, as mediated by deep muscle relaxation, may be seen as one important example in which the maladaptive anxiety response is being opposed by relaxation.

The preceding examples have illustrated inhibitions and phobic avoidances; conditioning techniques, however, have also been employed for the purpose of extinguishing obsessions, compulsive acts, and the like. In some instances, Wolpe has found the simple verbal command "Stop!" efficient in reducing obsessive ruminations; in others, self-administered electric shock has proven useful. Other forms of aversive conditioning have long been used in treating alcoholics who are injected with a drug which in combination with alcohol produces violent nausea. After a few experiences the patient becomes nauseated at the smell or even the sight of alcohol. Similarly, erotic fantasies in male homosexuals have been extinguished or reduced markedly by pairing their occurrence with electric shock. While often encouraging, the treatment results for this form of psychotherapy (as for others) are not unequivocal despite the claims of their proponents.

OPERANT CONDITIONING TECHNIQUES

Based on Skinner's learning theory, this form of behavior modification is designed to change the consequences of a given response. In general, the therapeutic aim is either to increase the likelihood that a response deemed desirable or adaptive will occur or to decrease the likelihood of deviant or maladaptive behavior. To accomplish this objective the therapist must bring the consequences of a given form of behavior under his control. Considerable success has been claimed for this approach in modifying patterns of behavior to which the patient seemingly clings with great tenacity and which have proven refractory to other therapeutic measures.

Salient examples may be found in the treatment of childhood autism (a form of severe withdrawal from human contacts), catatonic or stuporous behavior, slovenliness in chronic mental patients, and anorexia nervosa (severe refusal to eat, mostly found in adolescent girls and sometimes resulting in life-threatening weight loss). In a well-known study, Bachrach, Erwin, and Mohr (1965) successfully treated a female patient suffering from anorexia nervosa by pairing eating behavior with pleasurable experiences, such as visits from members of her family, watching television, and socializing with fellow patients, whereas they punished her for failing to eat. In order to link pleasurable consequences with socially desirable behavior it is necessary to attach punishment to the persistence of undesirable behavior.

To achieve behavior change the therapist frequently employs deprivations of various sorts to influence the patient's behavior. In treating autistic children, Lovaas (1965), for example, has occasionally used slapping and similar measures. In hospital settings, patients are often rewarded for "prosocial" behavior by tokens which can be exchanged for cigarettes, movie tickets, and other privileges. Entire wards in mental hospitals have been placed on a token economy system, reportedly with marked success. With children, candy and trinkets are often used as rewards.

Critical Assessment

ADVANTAGES

The advantages of behavior therapy as a set of techniques for modifying behavior (which, as we shall see, may not be equivalent to their theoretical value) may be summarized as follows:

1. The techniques are generally simple and easy to apply; therefore, the behavioral therapist does not require the degree of intensive and prolonged training usually demanded of dynamic (psychoanalytic) psychotherapists. This being the case, it is also possible to enlist the assistance of relatively untrained hospital personnel (e.g., psychiatric aides) and members of the patient's family in the therapeutic effort.

2. Behavioral techniques are aimed at the modification of *specific* forms of behavior; they are economical in terms of time, manpower, and cost, and the treatment outcomes are more easily measured. It is undeniable that this focus on empirical data and verification has had a salutary effect upon the field as a whole.

3. Since behavior therapy, unlike the dynamic therapies, makes considerably fewer demands on the patient's ability to verbalize his feelings, introspect, and communicate about his inner state, the techniques are applicable to many members of the population who traditionally have been considered unsuitable for psychotherapy. In par-

ticular, behavioral techniques are applicable to seriously disturbed (psychotic) hospital patients, poorly educated and culturally disadvantaged persons, all of whom are unable or unwilling to make long-term commitments to a traditional psychotherapeutic relationship, whose meaning and potential value they frequently fail to comprehend.

4. Behavior therapists have claimed success rates in excess of those reported by other therapists. Wolpe, for instance, has reported a success rate of 90 percent, and others have advanced similar claims. However, since most of the reported results are based on uncontrolled case studies and since comparisons between different forms of psychotherapy are still a problem (see Chapter 6), these success claims cannot be taken at face value. Nevertheless, the preponderance of the evidence indicates that behavioral techniques are effective in certain conditions, and their economy in terms of time, manpower, therapeutic effort, and cost constitutes a powerful argument in their favor.

CRITICISMS

One of the strongest appeals of behavior therapy has been the emphasis on empirical data and experimentation, thus upon the advancement of psychotherapy as a science. However, both the theoretical bases and the therapeutic claims of behavior therapy have come under critical attack (Breger & McGaugh, 1965). First, an important distinction must be made between the effectiveness of a technique and the adequacy of the theoretical model invoked to explain a given result. A technique for behavior change may work, but this proves little about the explanatory power of the theory to which it may be linked. This consideration is especially important because behavior therapists have attempted to defend the utility of their theoretical model in terms of their therapeutic claims. Apart from the effectiveness or outcome issue, two major criticisms may be distinguished: (1) the "science" issue; (2) the conception of neurosis, which also relates to the descriptive adequacy of behavioral techniques.

The "science" issue. Behavior therapists, as has been noted, have endeavored to link their work to the prestigious field of learning and the laboratory studies claimed to support these theories. The adequacy of the behavior therapists' theorizing thus is closely related to the adequacy of the learning theories to which they have recourse. While a discussion of the complex issues in this area far exceeds the scope of this volume, it seems appropriate to list briefly some of the major criticisms:

1. Existing learning theories do not adequately account for the acquisition of behavior in seemingly simple laboratory situations, and thus fail to do justice to the much more complex clinical phenomena with which the psychotherapist is necessarily concerned.

2. Terms like *stimulus, response, reinforcement,* and *conditioning,* have little precise meaning in behavior therapy. For example, "the imagination of a scene" can hardly be regarded as a rigorously defined stimulus, nor can "relaxation" be called a response except in a loose or metaphorical way. Hence the critics allege that terms which imply scientific respectability are employed by behavior therapists in ritualistic fashion to undergird a set of complex processes which they cannot possibly explain.

Psychologists have long searched for basic units, comparable to atoms in physics, to use as building blocks for their theories. For years it was believed that the Pavlovian conditioning model provided such a unit; however, it is now clear that it cannot serve this function. Rather than explaining the phenomena in the domain, the model raises more questions which in themselves are in need of explanation.

To illustrate: It has been shown that an animal—and to a greater extent a human organism—does not learn a simple response to a simple stimulus; instead he acquires a set of strategies of what needs to be done to reach a given objective. In the area of psycholinguistics, Chomsky (1959) has severely criticized Skinner's model of animal learning and asserted that it does not apply to complex learning in human beings. According to the psycholinguists, whose work may provide a more adequate model for learning in psychotherapy than classical or operant conditioning, a person learns a set of strategies or plans (grammar) which need not be and indeed often are not explicit. Similarly, the neurotic patient has learned certain maladaptive strategies to cope with stressful problems in his life, rather than specific responses to specific stimuli.

Another problem concerns the circularity in defining the term *reinforcement.* Critics have pointed out that the concept has no explanatory force but that it merely describes a state of affairs. In psychotherapy, it is extremely difficult to define what is being reinforced. All one typically notices is that behavior has changed as a result of a set of interventions which usually remain ill defined. Therefore, to assert that the behavior change has been due to reinforcement is begging the question.

In short, the "laws of learning" occupy a dubious status within the area of learning, and learning theorists have not succeeded in adequately explaining simple—much less complex—learning phenomena in the laboratory. Therefore, it is questionable whether the process of psychotherapeutic learning is illuminated by recourse to concepts which themselves are open to numerous criticisms.

Disregard of mediational variables. Perhaps the most potent argument that can be leveled against the behavior therapy position concerns the inadequate attention it accords central, mediational processes. Behavior therapists, as we have seen, equate the symptom with neurosis, eschewing central processes of which the symptom may be a function. Dynamic therapists believe that concepts referring to central processes such as motivation, repression, defense, etc., are indispensable, and their therapeutic efforts are basically directed at modifying the patient's inner state rather than his overt behavior, which is seen as consequent upon or flowing from the neurotic strategies the patient uses to cope with his "inner problems." One of Wolpe's (1960) own case descriptions, cited by Breger and McGaugh (1965), illustrates that in practice behavior therapists do not deal with single responses to single stimulus situations or conceive of the patient's difficulties in these terms:

> Case 5.—An attractive woman of 28 came for treatment because she was in acute distress as a result of her lovers' casual treatment of her. Every one of very numerous love affairs had followed a similar pattern —first she would attract the man, then she would offer herself on a platter. He would soon treat her with contempt and after a time leave her. In general she lacked assurance, was very dependent, and was practically never free from feelings of tension and anxiety [1960, p. 108].

Breger and McGaugh note that this description deals with a complex pattern of interpersonal strategies and central processes which in fact constitute what the dynamicist calls *neurosis*. The case description involves inferences from the observable data presented by the patient as symptoms and is not substantially different from a brief summary a psychoanalyst might produce.

Behavior therapists have contended that if the psychoanalytic view of neurosis is accepted, the removal of one symptom would require substitution by another. An enuretic child, for example, might use bed-wetting to express his resentment, dependency, and rebelliousness against his parents through this symptom. Once this symptom is treated without dealing with the alleged underlying cause, a new symptom would develop. The successful treatment of enuresis without the occurrence of symptom substitution is cited as evidence for the incorrectness of the dynamic hypothesis. This view represents an erroneous conception of dynamic theory (Weitzman, 1967), which allows for other forms of substitution besides gross symptoms.

As Wolpe's case history demonstrates, clinical data of neurotic processes do not fit the stimulus-response conditioning model but are much more in keeping with a position that allows for central processes. This is not to assert that psychoanalytic conceptions are beyond improvement, and one cannot dispute the utility of the techniques of behavior therapy in certain cases; what appears necessary is to avoid simplistic conceptions of highly complex phenomena. As Breger and McGaugh put it:

> To sum it up, it would seem that the behaviorists have reached a position where an inadequate conceptual framework forces them to adopt an inadequate and superficial view of the very data that they are concerned with. They are then forced to slip many of the key facts in the back door, so to speak, for example, when all sorts of fantasy, imaginary, and thought processes are blithely called responses. This process is, of course, parallel to what has gone on within S-R learning theory where all sorts of central and mediational processes have been cumbersomely handled with S-R terminology. Thus we have a situation where the behavior therapists argue strongly against a dynamic interpretation of neurosis at some points and at other points behave as if they had adopted such a point of view [1965, p. 350].

Suggested Readings

BANDURA, A.   Psychotherapy as a learning process. *Psychological Bulletin,* 1961, **58,** 143–159.

BREGER, L. & McGAUGH, J. L.   Critique and reformulation of "learning theory" approaches to psychotherapy and neurosis. *Psychological Bulletin,* 1965, **63,** 338–358.

EYSENCK, H. J.   *Behaviour therapy and the neuroses.* London: Pergamon, 1960.

EYSENCK, H. J.   (Ed.) *Experiments in behaviour therapy.* New York: Macmillan, 1964.

FRANKS, C. M.   (Ed.) *Behavior therapy: Appraisal and status.* New York: McGraw-Hill, 1969.

KRASNER, L., & ULLMANN, L. P.   *Research in behavior modification: New developments and implications.* New York: Holt, 1965.

ULLMANN, L. P. & KRASNER, L.   (Eds.) *Case studies in behavior modification.* New York: Holt, 1965.

WOLPE, J.   *Psychotherapy by reciprocal inhibition.* Stanford, Calif.: Stanford, 1958.

WOLPE, J.   *The practice of behavior therapy.* New York: Pergamon, 1969.

WOLPE, J., & LAZARUS, A. A.   *Behaviour therapy techniques. A guide to the treatment of neuroses.* London: Pergamon, 1966.

CHAPTER 5

OTHER FORMS OF
PSYCHOTHERAPY

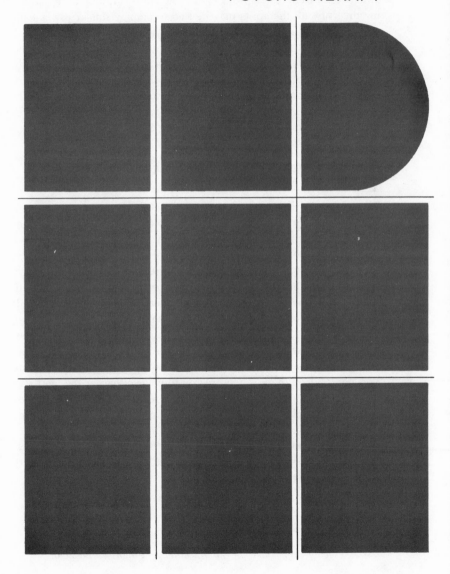

In the preceding chapters we have considered three major systems of *individual* psychotherapy. In addition to the ones described there are numerous variants, and there are others which proceed from different theoretical assumptions. In the final analysis there are almost as many psychotherapies as there are psychotherapists, since to a greater or lesser extent each develops his own style. However, despite this seeming diversity, all therapists may be said to employ similar psychological principles. In other words, the diversity in therapeutic techniques *as they are practiced* is probably far greater than allowed for in the schematic theoretical accounts; on the other hand, there are relatively few psychological principles employed by therapists of seemingly very different orientations. The degree of commonality or uniqueness of a given approach remains to be worked out, and it is fair to say that researchers have made only a bare beginning at this gargantuan task.

Additional Methods of Psychotherapy

This chapter will present thumbnail sketches of other representative forms of psychotherapy, including (1) group psychotherapy; (2) family psychotherapy; (3) child psychotherapy; and (4) certain innovative approaches. The variations and diversity of methods and techniques is truly staggering, and every year witnesses the appearance of new ones. Most of the work in these areas is being done by practicing clinicians, and the evidence is preponderantly based on clinical trials rather than on controlled research. In an applied area which has been rapidly evolving, this is to be expected, and there can be little question that almost any approach under the proper circumstances can point to successes. This does not mean that the dynamics are well understood; indeed there is good reason to believe that for the most part they are not. Partly for this reason the present volume is focused on individual psychotherapy with adults, for it is in the two-person (dyadic) relationship that by far the most important research has been carried out, and the probability of understanding the psychological processes at work in this setting appears to be potentially greater. Admittedly, this is the author's personal bias.

Group Psychotherapy

The rapid rise and growing popularity of group psychotherapy very probably reflect the emphasis of our society on group living. While it has been alleged that group psychotherapy tends to diminish further the value of the individual, the proponents assert that on the contrary the process of group therapy helps the individual to work out techniques for developing his own identity and for gaining a keener appreciation of the demands of group living as well as the opportunities it provides for self-development. Group psychotherapy is an experiment in group living, a technique for coming to terms with the problem of alienation and estrangement which pervades our society and which is one of the central problems in neurotic disorders. Another important argument in favor of group psychotherapy in contrast to individual psychotherapy is its greater economy in terms of time and professional manpower.

Group psychotherapy may be defined as "that form of therapy which is practiced by clinicians in groups formed for the specific purpose of helping individuals with their psychological and emotional difficulties, the depth of such therapy depending largely on the individual technique of the therapist" [Wolf, 1967, pp. 1234-1235].

PSYCHODRAMA

The beginnings of group therapy occurred simultaneously but independently in the United States and Austria in the early years of the twentieth century. Nevertheless, major credit for calling attention to the therapeutic potential inherent in small groups belongs to the Austrian psychiatrist J. L. Moreno (who later emigrated to the United States). Moreno began to experiment with what he termed the spontaneity theater, from which he developed the technique of psychodrama. Psychodrama is essentially a role-playing procedure intended to provide the patient with an "encounter," to encourage spontaneity, and to help him achieve a greater cognitive and emotional understanding of his maladaptive interpersonal behavior. The technique has been found particularly useful with patients whose ability to verbalize their feelings and experiences is limited, such as hospitalized schizophrenic patients, but its value has also been demonstrated with other groups.

PSYCHOANALYTIC GROUP PSYCHOTHERAPY

While differing in many respects from individual psychotherapy, analytic group therapy seeks to apply Freudian principles in the group setting. Pioneer work was done by S. R. Slavson in the United States around 1930, and originally the group technique was used with children between the ages of eight and fifteen.

As already indicated, group therapy is characterized by considerable diversity, depending as it does on the theoretical predilections of the practitioner. Some, for example, follow the classical Freudian model, while others prefer one of the more culturally oriented neo-Freudian variants. There are differences with respect to composition of the group, kinds of problems represented by the members of the group, extent to which group psychotherapy is combined with individual psychotherapy (by the group therapist or by another therapist), number of therapists conducting the group sessions (sometimes there is a co-therapist; sometimes there are group meetings without a therapist), etc. Typically, however, groups comprise seven to ten patients, and they meet in weekly sessions for 1½ to 2 hours. Patients are discouraged from social interactions outside of the group meetings, and they usually address each other only by their first names.

As is true of individual analytic therapy, analytic group therapy encourages the participants to engage in free association and exploration of their personal life histories and focuses on the understanding of unconscious processes through analysis of resistances and transference phenomena. Thus the emphasis rests on the individual, but there is the opportunity to study his interpersonal relations with other group members and to utilize this material for therapeutic purposes.

The therapist usually plays a relatively passive role, leaving the initiative with the group, intervening primarily to clarify neurotic patterns as they emerge in the group process and to handle crisis situations, such as the expression of hostile and destructive impulses by individuals toward other group members.

As therapy proceeds, group members become less dependent on the therapist as a parental authority figure, and they turn increasingly to their peers for support. There is, of course, the expectation that as the patient becomes more comfortable in relating to other group members, he will be able to apply the experience in his daily life and in turn become more flexible, independent, and self-respecting in his dealings with family and friends. Unlike individual psychotherapy, which has the advantage of working out in greater detail and depth the patient's problems in relation to one person, the group setting makes it possible for insights to occur in this unique context and for therapeutic learning to be applied immediately.

HUMAN RELATIONS TRAINING

During the last two decades, and more particularly in the 1960s, there has been a momentous growth in a wide variety of group experiences which may be loosely grouped under the heading of "human relations training." While no standard terminology has emerged, all forms of human relations training involve an intensive small-group experience of some kind. An additional problem in classifying these groups derives from the difficulty of differentiating between the purposes of *training* and *therapy*. In practice, there is often a considerable overlap, and the goal of behavior change is implicit even in groups which are ostensibly organized for the purpose of providing the participants with a significant emotional experience. Nevertheless, certain distinctions may be made between "therapy groups" and "training groups" (Bradford, Gibb, & Benne, 1964; Schein & Bennis, 1965).

Training groups, in contrast to therapy groups, emphasize the analysis of data emerging from the group interaction and are less concerned with etiology or historical antecedents of deviant behavior. The focus rests on personal growth, increased human potential, and self-realization instead of on the modification of maladaptive behavior. Interest lies in group processes, the functioning of the group, and interactions among group members instead of the psychodynamics of individual group members. Participants are encouraged to focus upon action, particularly in the group context, instead of working out solutions to individual problems (as occurs in individual psychotherapy). Finally, and perhaps most important, group members regard themselves as normal people who are interested in increasing their interpersonal effectiveness rather than as patients who approach a psychotherapist for the purpose of seeking amelioration of subjective distress.

Table 5-1 presents a sampling of different forms of human relations training, listed in decreasing order of therapeutic intent. Thus, creativity-growth groups and marathon groups resemble most closely traditional group psychotherapy, whereas inquiry groups and embedded groups shade into the area of education.

Groups designed to increase personal "growth" and "human potential" have achieved unprecedented popularity throughout the country in recent years and are avidly attended by people from many walks of life. "Growth centers," like Esalen Institute at Big Sur, California, sensitivity groups on many college campuses, and many others attract large numbers of people. Techniques frequently comprise a blending of traditional group psychotherapeutic methods with yoga, interpretive dance, psychedelic experiences, breathing exercises, nude encounters, and many others. Marathon groups which meet uninterruptedly from twenty-four to thirty-six hours have been found exceedingly powerful in mobilizing affect and mediating an emotional experience of considerable proportions in the participants.

In summary, group psychotherapy is an exceedingly broad field which currently enjoys tremendous popularity in the United States. It is characterized by extreme diffuseness, and in many respects has acquired the characteristics of a fad. While many of its practitioners are qualified psychotherapists, there are self-styled group leaders and trainers whose competence is exceedingly deficient and who are inadequately prepared to deal with emotional problems of individual group members. There can be no question that groups, whether they are called therapy groups, encounter groups, or any other name, may precipitate or potentiate latent neurotic, and at times psychotic, processes in the participants. Furthermore, "growth" experiences are frequently sought by persons with severe problems which may go unrecognized by unqualified trainers. A serious problem derives from the subtle confounding of "therapy" and "growth," and the fuzzy thinking generally pervading this area. Consequently anyone desirous of entering a group for whatever reason is well advised to assure himself concerning the qualifications of the leader or therapist.

Table 5-1 Categorization of Human Relations Training Treatments (Gibb, 1970)

Treatment designation	Central aims	Definitive activities or characteristics	Description
1. Creativity-growth	Creativity Awareness Releasing human potential	Induced experiences designed to expand human awareness	Otto & Mann (1968)
2. Marathon	Personal growth Greater capacity for being intimate	Uninterrupted interpersonal intimacy	Stoller (1968)
3. Emergent	Personal growth Group growth	Absence of leader Non-programmed, unpredictable, emergent activities	Gibb & Gibb (1968b)
4. Authenticity	Openness Authentic encounter	Interventions and experiences focused on openness and consonance	Bugental (1965)
5. Sensitivity	Personal competence Group effectiveness Organizational effectiveness	Focus on here-and-now experiences, and on group processes	Bradford, Gibb, & Benne (1964)
6. Programmed	Personal growth, and/or competence Group effectiveness Organizational effectiveness	Experiences initiated and/or directed by absent leaders	Berzon & Solomon (1966)
7. Microexperience	Interpersonal skills Group effectiveness Organizational effectiveness	Limited time (2 to 20 hours; 1 to 2½ days) Restricted depth	Bradford, Gibb, & Lippitt (1956)
8. Inquiry	Skills of inquiry Group effectiveness System effectiveness	Data gathering, quasi-structured experiences Focus on explicit and predictable individual and group learnings	Miles (1965)
9. Embedded	Team effectiveness Organizational effectiveness Problem-solving skills	Training experience embedded in sequential and continuous organization-based programs of inputs, data-gathering, and experiences	Argyris (1962) Friedlander (1968)

Family Therapy

Family therapy proceeds on the working assumption that the emotional problems of an individual are deeply rooted in his relationships to the members of his family as a major biosocial unit. Neurotic problems not only originate in the child's earliest relations with members of his family, but maladaptive patterns acquired in early childhood are frequently repeated at a later stage in the context of adult family living. Family therapy, therefore, is designed to involve all members of the patient's family, sometimes even grandparents. Its goals are to promote the adaptive capacities of the individual family members both as individuals and as members of the family, to resolve conflicts between the spouses and children, to foster an improved understanding between the generations, and to enable family members to achieve greater gratification of individual and family needs. Family therapy is a relatively recent development, and it is still in an experimental stage. Notable contributors have been Nathan Ackerman, Don Jackson, and Virginia Satir.

The therapist typically meets with the family as a unit and becomes a participant observer of the members' interaction. As he succeeds in establishing rapport and as therapy proceeds, he gains an understanding of the attitudes of the members toward each other, the prevailing climate within the family, and the manner in which the members cope with each other's needs, expectations, and demands. His knowledge of psychodynamic principles and his interpersonal skills enable him to isolate conflict-producing patterns and to confront the individual members with inconsistencies and contradictions between their verbal and nonverbal communications. He encourages them toward greater self-expression, freer communication, and openness with each other, and promotes their efforts to find viable solutions to their problems.

Family therapy appears to be an extraordinarily functional and rational approach to psychotherapy, and it capitalizes upon existing patterns of relationship in a natural group. Its value is probably greatest in families whose members have at least a modicum of loyalty to each other, where hostility and strife have not as yet become pervasive, and where individual members are not too severely incapacitated by their respective emotional problems.

Child Psychotherapy

INTRODUCTION

Psychotherapy with children, as is true of other forms, is largely a creation of the twentieth century. Freud is credited with having treated the first child patient, a five-year-old boy, Little Hans, who was suffering from several phobias. Interestingly (because it foreshadows some recent developments in enlisting the help of nonprofessional therapists), the therapy was carried out by the little boy's father, who consulted with Freud at regular intervals.

There are as many different forms of psychotherapy with children as there are with adults, and numerous groupings are possible. For example, it is possible to differentiate child psychotherapies in terms of (1) length (long-term psychotherapy or brief psychotherapy); (2) therapeutic techniques (persuasive, educative, interpretive, suggestive); (3) intensity (psychoanalysis versus numerous other forms); (4) emphasis on the psychodynamic viewpoint (typically referred to as "traditional") as opposed to learning approaches to psychotherapy (exemplified by conditioning methods); (5) theoretical concepts preferred by the therapists (e.g., Freud, Rank, Rogers); (6) therapeutic goals (changes in superego standards, identification with the therapist, achievement of increased ego control, behavior modification); and others. Any grouping is necessarily coarse and to some extent arbitrary. Furthermore, categories overlap, and their very definition is often a matter of dispute. These problems closely parallel the ones encountered in adult psychotherapy, and there is no standard method of psychotherapy with children any more than there is one in the case of adults.

DIFFERENCES BETWEEN ADULT AND CHILD PSYCHOTHERAPIES

Unlike the adult who is biologically (if not psychologically) independent, the child has a very real dependence on nurturing adults. Whereas the adult patient typically seeks therapeutic help of his own accord, implying at least a dim grasp of the nature of the problem, the child is brought to the private practitioner—or, more commonly, the child guidance clinic—by his parents. He has no appreciation of the difficulties for which the parents desire a solution, and he has no motivation to bring about changes.

Indeed, he often actively opposes the parents' decision that he needs therapy. As we have seen, the adult patient's motivation for therapy and his willingness to collaborate with the therapist are of primary importance. For these reasons, a significant part of the child therapist's effort, particularly in the early stages of therapy, must be designed to win the child's confidence. While an appeal to reason and rationality is at least of limited value with adult patients, it has very little utility with children. Furthermore, the child therapist must take account of the parents' part in the difficulties the child is experiencing. Not infrequently the child is cast in the patient role by parents who are oblivious to their own contribution to the child's problems. The therapist, therefore, often requires the parents themselves to seek therapy, often conducted in the context of groups comprised of parents whose children are in psychotherapy.

To the foregoing considerations must be added severe limitations in the child's ability to introspect, observe his own behavior, and verbalize his feelings. Rather than being able to take distance from himself, the child, to a greater extent than the average adult, expresses his feelings through actions. For these reasons, child therapy strongly stresses the need for a trusting relationship between the child and therapist, the latter being a person with whom the child can identify. Techniques which often work well with adults are unsuitable with children. Older children, of course, are capable of verbal communication to a certain extent, and as therapy progresses, they achieve greater competence in putting their feelings into words. These efforts are greatly aided by play activities and other spontaneous expressions, by means of which the therapist gains an understanding of the child's inner world, his conflicts, struggles, and frustrations.

DYNAMIC VERSUS LEARNING THEORY APPROACHES

The preceding emphasis on self-expression, self-exploration, analysis of defenses, interpretations of conflictual material, etc., is, of course, characteristic of psychoanalytic therapies and their variants. In contrast, the learning approaches to child therapy (see Chapter 4 on Behavior Therapy) deal more prominently with the regulation and control of conditions which serve as rewards or punishments for the child's behavior and which are seen as the raison d'être of maladaptive patterns. In addition, behavioral approaches stress learning by social imitation. This approach is well exemplified by the classical demonstration of Watson and Rayner (1920) almost half a century ago.

Little Albert was an eleven-month-old child who demonstrably was not afraid of white rats or other furry objects. Whenever Albert approached a white rat, the experimenter made a loud noise. After a few repetitions, Albert appeared fearful of white rats, and the phobia had generalized to rabbits and other furry objects. This reaction pattern persisted for several months. A few years later, another investigator (M. C. Jones, 1924) was able to show that a conditioned phobia of the kind just described could be eliminated by conditioning and social-imitation techniques.

Behavioral techniques have become increasingly popular in recent years, particularly in the treatment of conditions which have proven refractory to other approaches. Typical examples include: enuresis (bed wetting); school phobias; learning disabilities based on emotional factors; and autism.

Lang (1969) reported the treatment of a nine-month-old infant who for unknown reasons had developed a vomiting response to food intake. The child was normal in other respects, but the problem had resulted in severe weight loss which began to threaten the child's life. Despite careful investigation, no precipitating factors could be found in the child's relationship to his parents. The method employed by Lang consisted of aversive conditioning in the form of electric shocks as soon as the vomiting response, which had been carefully monitored by the experimenter, occurred. According to Lang, vomiting ceased after a few repetitions, and the child experienced no further feeding difficulties thereafter.

While behavioral techniques are never concerned with the child as a "total person," and their approach is symptom oriented, considerable sophistication and ingenuity have been brought to bear by numerous investigators.

RÉSUMÉ

Child therapy appears to be indicated in many instances where parental techniques of child-rearing (sometimes in combination with organic deficiencies and malfunctions) have resulted in marked maladaptations in the child. Early problems frequently become exacerbated when the child enters school and comes to the attention of authorities through, for example, aggressive behavior which disrupts classroom discipline or interferes with the educational process. The therapeutic approach to child treatment varies in accordance with a wide variety of factors, including the therapist's theoretical orientation and goals. Because of the child's close and continuing relationship with his parents, the therapist usually attempts to secure the parents' collaboration, either by making them his allies or by inducing them to modify their own attitudes and feelings in relation to each other and the child, a task which ordinarily requires the parents to obtain therapeutic help or counseling themselves. While the child's unique situation as an integral member of the family poses special problems for therapy, there are also significant advantages in the treatment of children as opposed to adults. These can be found in the child's greater potential for growth and change and his malleability and openness to influence, which have not as yet been transformed into the kind of extensive rigidity and resistance to change frequently encountered in adults. With respect to the problem of evaluating treatment outcomes (see Chapters 6 and 7), the difficulties are complex. In addition, the researcher is faced with the possibility that changes observed as a function of therapeutic interventions might have occurred as a function of maturation. The common observation that children seemingly outgrow some problems, which may turn out to be a function of a particular developmental phase, illustrates the point.

In addition to individual psychotherapy, numerous other approaches are being employed in treating emotional problems in children. Residential treatment centers, group psychotherapy, and other experiences in group living are being employed with promising results. Efforts are also being made to identify incipient problems before they become severe and to prevent the occurrence of difficulties through educational work with parents.

Innovative Approaches

In this concluding section brief mention will be made of recent departures which illustrate the increasing concern of psychotherapists and other professionals with the great social problems confronting our society today. Most of this work is at a very early stage of development, and thorough evaluations of its merit remain to be carried out. In a very real sense it is applied science since it is concerned with the translation of traditional psychotherapeutic principles, imperfect as they are, to new settings and new problems.

As early as 1917 Freud foresaw that the psychotherapy of the future, as he conceived it, would be an amalgam of "the pure gold of psychoanalysis with baser metals," the latter term referring to such techniques as suggestion, persuasion, and the like. This recommendation was based on his recognition that the two-person psychoanalytic relationship, regardless of how many therapists might be trained, would never be sufficient to meet the needs of society for psychotherapeutic services. He also realized that governments eventually would have to take active steps to create treatment centers and subsidize their services to make them available to a wider band of the population.

While mental hygiene clinics came into being in the second quarter of this century, and the team approach (involving the professions of psychiatry, clinical psychology, and psychiatric social work) began to make some inroads on the nation's mental health problem, major impetus came in the 1950s through legislative efforts by the federal government. Congress appointed a Joint Commission of Mental Illness and Health, which in 1957 published a set of recommendations, many of which, however, were not implemented. Perhaps greater influence was exerted by the National Institute of Mental Health, which was instrumental in funding community mental health centers throughout the country, stimulating experimental approaches and demonstration projects, and supporting research on a major scale.

These developments were based on a growing appreciation that traditional psychotherapy had been a luxury available only to the relatively affluent members of society, and that few if any services were available to the poor and disadvantaged citizens. These facts were heavily underscored by an important study by Hollingshead and Redlich (1958) which provided concrete evidence that members of the upper classes, regardless of the nature of the disorder, were typically able to command the services of highly trained private practitioners, whereas lower class individuals were usually treated in state mental institutions, the treatment consisting largely of custodial care and tranquilizing drugs. In other words, the form and quality of psychotherapeutic services was shown to be a function of social class membership rather than of the kind of distress for which help was needed. While no radical solutions to this problem have been forthcoming, it is true that lower class and culturally deprived individuals now have a greater chance of getting some form of psychotherapeutic help. In part, this goal has been achieved through the creation of new treatment centers in the community and through recruitment of nonprofessional personnel, to whom highly trained professionals serve as consultants. In pursuing this objective it has been found that a much larger number of individuals than had previously been realized can function in therapeutic roles, and that self-help efforts by various groups can similarly serve a therapeutic purpose. Whether this new manpower pool, achieved in part through dilution of available resources, can become a viable therapeutic force remains to be seen, but contemporary efforts in this area are vigorous, bold, and often imaginative.

The following examples are illustrative of these trends: Rioch, Elkes, Flint, Usdansky, Newman, and Silber (1963) trained a small group of housewives to function as adjunct therapists in mental-hygiene clinics. The women were well educated and received comprehensive training in psychopathology and psychotherapeutic principles. Furthermore, they had been carefully selected. Subsequent experience demonstrated that they were able to function effectively under supervision. Another investigator, Gould (1967), working closely with a labor union, adapted his psychotherapeutic approach to treating blue-collar workers. Slack (1960) succeeded in carrying out psychotherapy with a group of juvenile delinquents who were initially unmotivated for such work. He was able to enlist their cooperation by paying them a small fee for participating in his project, whose primary purpose had been disguised. In a variety of settings nonprofessionals (some of whom had been patients themselves) have been trained to function as psychotherapists with lower class patients. In community mental health clinics, psychologists have worked with school principals, guidance counselors, ministers, etc., by training them to cope directly with crisis situations involving the people with whom they normally work, instead of referring them to a treatment agency. Crisis call centers, suicide-prevention centers, and walk-in clinics have been designed to provide prompt service to people in acute distress at a time when their need for help is greatest. Behavior modification principles have been successfully employed in mental hospital settings by motivating patients to engage in "prosocial" responses (self-care, productive use of time, etc.) through the selective distribution of tokens exchangeable for cigarettes, candy, movie passes, and other privileges ("token economies"). Other efforts, aimed at restoring chronic hospitalized patients to social roles in the community, have taken the form of "halfway houses," that is, way stations between the hospital and the community in which an intermediate amount of encouragement, supervision, and guidance is extended to patients for whom hospitalization is no longer mandatory.

In these treatment programs, as can readily be seen, psychotherapy is not employed as a precision tool—perhaps this can never be done in any case—and many approaches may be more appropriately described as a form of social intervention than as psychotherapy in a strict sense. While these approaches are responsive to the needs of society and of undoubted social value, it may be questioned whether in and of themselves they can advance the scientific understanding of psychological change. While it would be premature to judge their promise in this regard, the task of isolating and defining the psychological forces at work may fall to the researcher rather than the practitioners or the agents of social change.

Summary

This chapter has provided a brief overview of a variety of therapeutic techniques which in one form or another depart from the two-person (dyadic) relationship which forms the basis of modern psychotherapy and to which major attention has been given in preceding chapters.

Brief descriptions have been given of group psychotherapy, family therapy, child psychotherapy, and a set of innovative approaches which can be grouped only in a loose way.

These approaches have come into being partly as a response to growing social needs and partly as a search for techniques which might be more effective in dealing with special populations and problems for which individual psychotherapy had been seen as being of limited usefulness.

The theoretical bases and the conceptual frameworks of most techniques discussed in this chapter are as yet insufficiently developed, and their justification is demonstrated largely by clinical use rather than by trustworthy research evidence.

Suggested Readings

ACKERMAN, N. W. *The psychodynamics of family life*. New York: Basic Books, 1958.

BACH, G. R. *Intensive group psychotherapy*. New York: Ronald Press, 1954.

BOSZSORMENYI-NAGY, I., & FRAMO, J. L. (Eds.) *Intensive family therapy*. New York: Hoeber-Harper, 1965.

BRADFORD, L. P., GIBB, J. R., & BENNE, K. D. *T group theory and laboratory method*. New York: Wiley, 1964.

BUGENTAL, J. F. T. *The search for authenticity*. New York: Holt, 1965.

OTTO, H. A., & MANN, J. *Ways of growth: Approaches to expanding awareness*. New York: Grossman, 1968.

SATIR, V. *Conjoint family therapy*. Palo Alto, Calif.: Science and Behavior Books, 1964.

SCHEIN, E. H., & BENNIS, W. G. *Personal and organizational change through group methods*. New York: Wiley, 1965.

SCHUTZ, W. C. *Joy: Expanding human awareness*. New York: Grove Press, 1967.

SLAVSON, S. R. *Textbook in analytic group psychotherapy*. New York: International Universities Press, 1964.

WESCHLER, I. R., & REISEL, J. *Inside a sensitivity training group*.

Los Angeles: Institute of Industrial Relations, University of California, Los Angeles, 1958.

WHITAKER, D. S., & LIEBERMAN, M. A. *Psychotherapy through the group process*. New York: Atherton, 1964.

WOLF, A., & SCHWARTZ, E. K. *Psychoanalysis in groups*. New York: Grune and Stratton, 1962.

CHAPTER 6

PROBLEMS OF RESEARCH

Introduction

With the advent of psychotherapy as a recognized professional activity in the twentieth century, psychotherapists have amassed a large body of clinical observations, and much of what we know about the area is based upon this work. Naturalistic observation in any science is a legitimate method for advancing knowledge, and in areas in which controlled experiments cannot be carried out it is the only method of inquiry. Often naturalistic observation represents an early stage in the development of science and is gradually superseded by laboratory experimentation in which variables can be isolated and systematically varied while others are rigorously controlled. In complex areas, such as psychotherapy, where a host of variables interact, such control is extremely difficult to achieve, and it is this complexity which has greatly hindered research progress. The problems impeding objective research will be examined presently in greater detail. Psychotherapists, of course, are convinced that their preferred techniques are effective. But despite efforts at objectivity, the possibilities of human error are great, particularly when there is a deep personal involvement, which is typically the case when a patient and a therapist meet over an extended period of time. Nor can anyone be certain that changes in the patient's behavior are a function of the interventions to which the therapist attributes them. To clarify these problems, investigators have devoted considerable effort to research during the last two or three decades. Beginning in 1958, three national conferences have been convened (Rubinstein & Parloff, 1959; Strupp & Luborsky, 1962; Shlien, Hunt, Matarazzo, & Savage, 1968) to deal with these issues. Since the practice of psychotherapy as an applied art has great social implications, research in this area far transcends a pure scientific interest.

In essence, research in psychotherapy is concerned with the question of personality and behavior change as a function of a planful interpersonal experience, called psychotherapy. Suppose a person in distress enters psychotherapy at Point A (Figure 6-1) and is seen by a trained psychotherapist in regular sessions over a period of time. When therapy is terminated at Point B, one needs to answer these

Fig. 6-1 *Schematic presentation of the therapy sequence.*

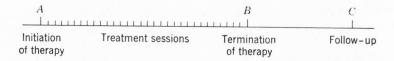

questions: Has the patient changed demonstrably over the time span in which psychotherapy has occurred? If so, what is the nature of the changes? Can these changes be reasonably attributed to the therapist's interventions? Are the changes lasting so that a sustained effect can be demonstrated at a subsequent follow-up (Point C)?

In principle, these questions are straightforward and not intrinsically different from those asked by researchers in other areas of science in which one wishes to assess the effect of a specified experimental treatment. A simple experimental design frequently employed in scientific research involves the comparison of two groups, one of which receives the treatment under investigation whereas the other (designated as "control group") does not. If all other variables have been held constant, resulting differences between two groups can then be attributed to the experimental manipulation.

Suppose an investigator wishes to determine whether a given form of psychotherapy is effective with phobic disorders. For this purpose he may set up a simple experimental design, as follows:

| Experimental Group A | Initial assessment | Treatment | Final assessment |
| Control Group B | Initial assessment | No treatment | Final assessment |

If the groups are comparable and if the treatment can be adequately defined, measurable differences in outcome favoring the experimental group would constitute evidence for the effectiveness of the treatment. The simplicity of this design (or any other, for that matter), as we shall presently see, is highly deceptive. For the sake of convenience, it is useful to consider the variables encountered by the researcher under the headings of (1) patient; (2) situational; and (3) treatment.

Patient Variables

In order to determine whether the members of experimental group A are comparable to those of control group B it is indispensable to carry out a psychological assessment. To accomplish this objective we must first decide *which measures are relevant;* second, we must have *techniques for measuring adequately what we want to assess;* finally, and related to the foregoing, we must have *measures which are sufficiently reliable and valid to enable us to demonstrate changes (or their absence) over time.* Unless these stipulations are met, any descriptions of improvement will remain unconvincing because they are not anchored to any definable points. In the above example, we must have measures to help us ascertain that the two groups are comparable at the beginning of the experiment, and our yardsticks must be sufficiently precise, so that we can carry out an assessment at the end of therapy for the purpose of evaluating the effectiveness of the therapeutic interventions.

Granting these requirements, the next problem concerns the selection of those variables which, singly or in combination, may be affected by psychotherapeutic interventions. Here one enters a field of research which is beset with its own complex difficulties.

Traditional diagnostic labels (*hysteria, phobia, anxiety state,* etc.) convey a certain amount of information about a patient, but they are crude and invariably involve a great deal of overlap. Patients' self-reports, whether elicited in an interview or through objective tests, cannot be taken at face value; they often call for clinical inferences concerning which there exists much controversy. Projective techniques reveal useful information about the patient's inner world, but their reliability and validity is open to question on numerous grounds. The symptoms a patient presents may be reasonably concrete and specific (as in the case of a phobia), yet more typically patients complain of a variety of disturbances, such as anxiety and depression—states about whose meaning in the total context of the patient's life clinical observers will often disagree. Some clinicians, as we have seen, view symptoms as the manifestation of unconscious conflicts; others reject dynamic concepts and are willing to equate the symptom with the neurotic disorder. Furthermore, a patient's status is by no means stable; it may change from day to day, sometimes even from hour to hour. The manner in which a patient's problem is conceptualized is frequently a function of the clinician's theoretical presuppositions, so that the person of the evaluator becomes a highly important variable. It has been shown (Sandifer, Hordern, Timbury, & Green, 1968) that even experienced clinicians, viewing films of initial interviews, often agree poorly on a diagnosis.

Next, what respective weights are to be given to maladaptive behaviors and subjective feelings? Symptoms, clearly, are not additive, but how can they be combined into a meaningful whole? How can the personalities and behavior patterns of two individuals be compared and equated? Apart from assessments of the patient's current functioning, it is exceedingly important to take into account his reasons for entering therapy, his motivation for desiring change, his intelligence, age, education, social class, ability to verbalize and communicate his feelings—all of which have been shown to have a bearing on therapeutic outcomes. In our example, these assessments are essential to determine whether patients who are assigned to experimental and control groups are comparable (homogeneous).

While in no way exhaustive, the foregoing list conveys a sense of the great difficulties facing the researcher who desires to assess a patient's personality and behavior. Clearly, if assessments are fluid and ambiguous at the beginning of therapy, they cannot be more precise upon termination or at any other time. This statement merely illustrates the point that it is manifestly impossible to compare readings on a rubber yardstick.

However, even if accurate assessments at the beginning and at the end of psychotherapy can be made, we are still faced with the problem of deciding whether a particular change constitutes *improvement*. If a group of plants, as a result of exposure to a new fertilizer, grows 2 inches taller than an untreated group, this is an objective fact, although the researcher may still have to determine whether it is a desirable outcome. In psychotherapy research we face considerably greater difficulties in (1) measuring changes and (2) evaluating the character of the changes.

In our example, the criterion of improvement (outcome) would be disappearance or diminution of the patients' phobias. If all patients in our experimental and control groups suffered from a fear of heights, we would credit the psychotherapy with curative powers if the patients in the experimental group, following psychotherapy, were no longer fearful of high places whereas the control group remained unchanged. Such a change could be measured by (a) the patient's self-report; (b) observations of his behavior, such as whether he avoids high places; (c) psychophysiological measures when he is in a high place, such as sweating, and palpitations; (d) reports by members of his family or friends; (e) the therapist's judgment. All these measures, singly or in combination, have in fact been employed in various outcome studies. A distinction has often been made between *subjective* measures (for example, the patient's self-report of his feelings), which of course are subject to conscious or unconscious distortions, and *objective* measures (for example, observations by external observers) of the patient's behavior. In American psychology, objective or behavioral measures have generally been considered superior to subjective ones, largely because they lend themselves more readily to quantification and comparison.

In our hypothetical study the investigator might have specified that his criterion of improvement is a reduction in the patient's avoidance behavior, that is, disappearance of the symptom. If the treatment to which the experimental patients were exposed had been behavior therapy, the therapists would probably accept the investigator's criterion, although they would also want the patient to feel more comfortable and less anxious in the previously feared situations. Dynamically oriented therapists might reject the behavioral criterion as insufficient and point out that the phobic symptom is merely a surface manifestation of the patient's underlying dependency, which the treatment had left untouched. Be that as it may, as long as a criterion of improvement has been specified in advance, regardless of whether therapists following different orientations agree to it, the result must be accepted on its own terms. In many studies, unfortunately, no consensus about outcome criteria was reached, and, worse, different forms of therapy aimed at widely divergent outcomes have often been compared. (See the illustrative study later in this chapter.) In the present example, an assessment of whether the treated patients are now emotionally more mature than the control group obviously calls for different evaluations than observations of their behavior, although it would be undeniable that their behavior had been modified.

One of the troubles with phobias, as with any other symptom, is the fact that they rarely occur alone. A patient suffering from a fear of heights usually suffers from other anxieties and problems in living which may emerge in the course of the treatment, although he may present a particular symptom as the problem. In other words, the typical psychotherapist does not treat single symptoms, but he deals with persons whose lives are disordered in a variety of ways. In a person who has difficulties in getting along with his spouse, suffers from recurrent headaches and depressions, and exhibits a variety of complaints in addition to a fear of heights, amelioration of the last symptom may well be a trivial accomplishment. This is one important reason why many psychotherapists (and researchers) insist on considering the totality of the patient's living and reject what they consider an overemphasis upon symptoms.

If one wishes to extend the assessment to the patient's total life situation, he encounters other problems which usually involve complex value judgments. Suppose one of our phobic patients, as a result of therapy, becomes more assertive with his wife and with his boss. The patient may feel better because he is less fearful of standing up for his rights, but the other people in his life may experience him as more troublesome, and his changed behavior may challenge their own domineering tendencies. From the patient's (and perhaps the therapist's) standpoint the changes may be viewed as improvements; from the vantage point of the wife or the boss, the patient has become cantankerous and quarrelsome. Whose judgment is to be accepted? Which behavior is more desirable in the broader context of society? Another phobic patient in our sample may become more independent and consequently reject the "helping" attitudes of other members in his family. In this instance the patient's behavior may not be seen as troublesome by other people in his life, but they in turn may feel frustrated because he no longer satisfies their own needs. Again, the evaluative problem has become complicated. Examples could be multiplied, but it can be appreciated that the patient's behavior must be viewed in interaction with his milieu, and changes in one sphere of the patient's feelings and attitudes will inevitably have reverberations in other facets of his personality. Therefore, it is now being conceded that therapeutic changes are multidimensional and that they cannot be generalized. What constitutes improvement in one person may be seen as deterioration in another, and group comparisons are at best a risky undertaking.

Situational Variables Inducing Behavior Changes

Unlike laboratory animals which may be isolated in cages for the duration of an experiment in order to control their environment, human beings are continually exposed to a wide variety of influences, of which psychotherapy is only one. Even when a patient is seen in psychotherapy five times a week for an hour each time, there are 163 uncontrolled hours during that same week. Researchers cannot disregard this large block of time, nor can one readily assume that, for a given sample of persons, the extra-therapy experience will be approximately equal. The point to be made is that *a good research study must present concrete evidence that changes occurring in a patient are largely due to the influence of psychotherapy rather than to extraneous factors.*

There are many ways in which extra-therapy variables may influence patient change. For example, there may be "spontaneous" improvements without any formal psychotherapy, and since patients tend to apply for therapy when they are in a state of crisis, some improvement may be expected even if no therapy had been undertaken. However, there are additional problems. For example: patients marry or they obtain a divorce; they change jobs; they grow older and perhaps mature psychologically as well as biologically; they get lucky breaks or experience adversity; they may make new friends or lose old ones; they may join a church or a civic organization; they may develop physical ailments. To complicate matters, beneficial changes in some patients' life situations which may be the direct result of psychotherapy, in others may be fortuitous; yet there are no good techniques for keeping the two apart. Thus it is clear that situational variables may greatly interfere with efforts to demonstrate the effectiveness of psychotherapy.

THE NO-TREATMENT CONTROL GROUP

Frank (1959) suggests as a possible solution to this difficulty the use of an equivalent *no-treatment control group* to be compared with a group of patients who undergo psychotherapy. If the therapy group did better, one might have grounds for believing that the experience of therapy accounts for the difference. Unfortunately, selection of truly equivalent samples confronts the investigator with the problems which have already been considered under patient variables. But assuming an approximation to true equivalence is possible, there are special problems relating to a no-treatment control group.

A major problem, as Frank points out, is that an adequate no-therapy control group would have to be studied for the same length of time as the experimental group. This would be necessary to allow for the occurrence of comparable extra-therapy life experiences. For various reasons, however, a control group composed of normal subjects —that is, individuals who are not in distress and desirous of professional help—is largely meaningless. Furthermore, the special attention accorded such individuals by a research team may influence their responses to questionnaires and tests.

As an alternative, one might wish to form a control group from patients who apply for help to a clinic. This course of action presents the investigator with the ethical problem of withholding help from people who need it and to whom presumably it would be available were it not for the stipulations of the experiment. Private practitioners or clinics can hardly justify such procedures to themselves and the community. As it happens, most clinics, by dint of necessity, do have waiting lists; however, there is evidence to show that patients promptly accepted for therapy often differ in important respects from individuals placed on the waiting list. Moreover, patients who feel they need professional help will often seek it elsewhere if they cannot get it from a clinic or therapist in private practice. For example, they may seek out physicians, ministers, or turn to friends. As Frank cogently observes, accepting a patient for psychotherapy is one form of an interpersonal relationship; refusing treatment is another. In the latter case, patients often feel rejected, and thus the experience cannot be regarded as neutral.

THE CONTROL GROUP

A more promising approach might be to offer the *control group* a form of psychotherapy which differs in significant respects from the method of treatment to be studied, or to offer such individuals minimum contacts with a professional person. The objection here is that the essential ingredients of psychotherapy have not been well defined. However, on practical grounds this alternative may be the least objectionable.

Problems in Defining Psychotherapy

PSYCHOTHERAPY NOT A UNITARY PROCESS

Among the most serious problems in psychotherapy research is the definition of psychotherapy—the independent variable whose effects we wish to assess. If one is interested in studying the efficacy of a pharmacological agent, the chemical composition of the drug is usually known, and dosage can be systematically varied. Although in many published reports psychotherapy has been studied as analogous to a uniform and constant method of influence, this assumption is not warranted. To illustrate, some decades ago it was assumed that psychoanalysis consisted of a clearly specifiable set of operations, including the fostering of a transference neurosis, interpretations of resistances, etc. It became clear (Glover, 1938), however, that the techniques employed even by highly experienced analysts whose training presumably had been quite homogeneous differed widely in almost every respect. Furthermore, it has proven extremely difficult to define the nature and extent of differences in technique, chiefly because the major dimensions of any therapeutic technique are not known.

TECHNIQUE AND THE PERSON OF THE THERAPIST

It must also be borne in mind that no psychotherapeutic technique is applied in a vacuum, and techniques are almost inextricably intertwined with the personality of the therapist. Moreover, psychotherapy unavoidably involves a complex set of interpersonal interactions between a patient and a therapist, and the techniques to which the latter may attribute his therapeutic effectiveness may not be the crucial aspect of their interaction. In fact, *we have as yet no convincing demonstrations that the outcomes of a given form of psychother-*

apy are exclusively, or even largely, a function of the techniques employed by the therapist. As Frank put it:

> The most important, and unfortunately the least understood, situational variable in psychotherapy is the therapist himself. His personality pervades any technique he may use, and because of the patient's dependence on him for help, he may influence the patient through subtle cues of which he may not be aware. Dr. David Rioch tells an amusing example of a patient of his who was always depressed in the treatment interviews except on five occasions when he seemed quite bright and alert. This puzzled Dr. Rioch until he reviewed his notes and realizing that on these five mornings, and on no others, he himself had taken benzedrene [1959, p. 17].

The study of therapeutic techniques, including attempts to define and quantify them, and research on the personality of therapist have become important areas of inquiry in their own right. Pertinent research will be reviewed in a later section. In the present context it is sufficient to observe that comparisons between different forms of psychotherapy are virtually impossible until their respective components can be defined. Differences in therapeutic outcomes, even by the same therapist, may be due to the *therapist's personality*—that is, the manner in which the therapist as a person interacts with a given patient—rather than to treatment variables. While not a likely possibility, it is certainly conceivable that the therapist's personal attributes may be a more potent force than any technique he might deliberately employ. Undoubtedly it will prove difficult to analyze these two components, but we can be reasonably sure that the total therapeutic influence consists of both sets of factors in varying combinations.

The problems encountered by researchers in this area and the persistence of controversy may be illustrated by reference to two typical studies whose major focus rests on the assessment of therapeutic outcomes.

Two Illustrative Studies

1. DOES PSYCHOTHERAPY HELP?: EYSENCK'S RESEARCH

In 1952 H. J. Eysenck, a British psychologist, startled psychotherapists and researchers (not to mention patients and the public at large) with a study whose results were interpreted to cast serious question upon the efficacy of individual psychotherapy in general and psychoanalysis in particular.

In order to make any meaningful statements about the effects of psychotherapy, Eysenck reasoned, it is necessary to compare psychotherapy patients with untreated controls. The effects of psychotherapy, if any, would thus be demonstrated in terms of differences between the two major groups. The base line was provided by two studies, one dealing with the percentage of neurotic patients discharged annually from New York state hospitals as recovered or improved, the other a survey of 500 patients who presented insurance claims based on neurotic disabilities. The latter group did not receive formal psychotherapy but was treated with sedatives and the like by general practitioners. The crucial assumption in these two studies was that the patients did not receive psychotherapy.

Typical criteria of recovery were: (1) return to work and ability to carry on well in economic adjustments for at least a five-year period; (2) no further complaint or very slight difficulties; (3) making of successful social adjustments.

The results of these studies were compared by Eysenck with nineteen reports in the literature dealing with the outcomes of both psychoanalytic and eclectic types of psychotherapy. Pooling the results he found that patients treated by means of psychoanalysis improved to the extent of 44 percent; patients treated eclectically improved to the extent of 64 percent; patients treated only custodially or by general practitioners (the control groups) improved to the extent of 72 percent.

Since the most intensive, ambitious, and thoroughgoing form of psychotherapy is presumably practiced at psychoanalytic treatment centers, Eysenck's results under this heading are particularly instructive. Table 6-1 presents the data which were abstracted from published reports.

Eysenck presented his tabulation of results from therapy under four headings: (1) cured, or much improved; (2) improved; (3) slightly improved; (4) not improved, died, discontinued treatment, etc. It may be seen that some 21 percent of the patients treated were only "slightly improved" and 35 percent fell into the limbo category "not improved, died, discontinued treatment, etc."

Eysenck indicated that in this tabulation he classed those who stopped treatment with those who were rated as not improved. This seemed reasonable to him on the ground that a patient who failed to finish treatment should be considered a therapeutic failure. However, if only those patients are considered who completed therapy—about one-third broke off treatment—the percentage of successful treatments rises to about 66 percent (Eysenck). Bergin (1970) has carefully re-analyzed the data in the studies used by Eysenck and concluded that they are open to interpretations other than those chosen by Eysenck. For example, Bergin (not a proponent of psychoanalysis) states that from the data reported by the Berlin Psychoanalytic Institute one can derive an improvement rate of 91 percent with as much justification as the 39 percent rate computed by Eysenck. He notes: "I can see no clear justification for choosing one interpretation over another, even though I do have personal biases in certain directions. The ambiguity in these data cannot be resolved." And further: "It is of particular interest . . . that the longer and more intensive the treatment, the better the results."

From the comparisons between treatment and control groups, Eysenck concluded that "roughly two-thirds of a group of neurotic patients will recover or improve to a marked extent within about two years of the onset of their illness, whether they are treated by means of psychotherapy or not" [p. 322]. In a more recent critique, Eysenck (1961) reaffirmed his conclusion that "neurotic disorders tend to be self-limiting, that psychoanalysis is no more successful than any other method, and that in fact all methods of psychotherapy fail to improve on the recovery rate obtained through ordinary life experiences and nonspecific treatment." However, he went beyond the earlier assertions by stating: "What is even more conclusive, we have found that there is strong evidence to suggest that short methods of treatment based on an alternative hypothesis (learning theory) are significantly more successful in treating neurotic disorders than is psychotherapy of the psychoanalytic type" [p. 721]. Consequently, he advocated that the psychoanalytic model be discarded.

EYSENCK'S CRITICS REPLY

As might be expected, Eysenck's serious indictment of psychotherapy evoked heated discussions, numerous writers (e.g., Luborsky, 1954;

Table 6–1 Summary of Reports of the Results of Psychotherapy (From Eysenck, 1952)

Report	N	Cured; much improved	Improved	Slightly improved	Not improved; died; left treatment	Percent cured; much improved; improved
(A) Psychoanalytic [*]						
1. Fenichel (1930; pp. 28–40)	484	104	84	99	197	39
2. Kessel & Hyman (1933)	34	16	5	4	9	62
3. Jones (1936; pp. 12–14)	59	20	8	28	3	47
4. Alexander (1937; pp. 30–43)	141	28	42	23	48	50
5. Knight (1941)	42	8	20	7	7	67
All cases	760	335		425		44%

[*] Part B (Eclectic) omitted.

Rosenzweig, 1954; Strupp, 1963) taking issue with the study and questioning Eysenck's sweeping conclusions. Major criticisms will be discussed under the following headings.

1. Inadequacy of the control groups. It may be seen that the weight of Eysenck's argument rests on the untreated control groups. In other words, if the "spontaneous recovery rate" is significantly less than the reported 72 percent, the improvement figures for formal psychotherapy would command greater respect. Bergin (1970) regards this figure as grossly inflated.

As noted earlier in this chapter, a control group must be comparable to a treatment group *in most significant respects* with the exception of the independent variable (in this case psychotherapy) whose effects are to be assessed. Eysenck of course recognized that in a strict sense his control groups were deficient, but he asserted that the control patients were as seriously disturbed as the treatment patients and that the standards of recovery were equally stringent in both instances. Both assumptions appear unjustified.

First, neurotic patients are not usually admitted to state mental hospitals, and undoubtedly they constitute a rather unusual group. The statement that they did not receive any formal psychotherapeutic treatment can probably be accepted, except that the helpful attitudes of the hospital staff and situational changes may have exerted nonspecific beneficial effects. However, it is virtually certain that they differed from the patients who were seen in psychoanalysis in such important respects as education, socioeconomic status, motivation for therapy, etc. Similar strictures apply to the second control group which consisted of outpatients who received insurance benefits on account of their neurotic disabilities. They, too, undoubtedly differed markedly from the patients in the treated groups. While apparently they did not receive formal psychotherapy, they were seen by general medical practitioners who, in addition to prescribing sedatives, undoubtedly listened sympathetically to their complaints, very probably offered reassurance, advice, and encouragement—factors concerning which no information was provided.

Assessments of outcome aside (see below), there can be little question that the control and treatment groups were far from comparable, therefore invalidating their use for the purpose intended by Eysenck.

2. *Faulty measures of outcome.* From the reports of the psychoanalytic institutes which Eysenck used in his research one judges that the patients were very carefully selected and the outcome of their therapy was judged by rigorous standards. To be sure, evaluations were made by the treating therapists (although often in consultation with other members of the clinic staff) who cannot be regarded as unbiased observers. Furthermore, if a therapist has invested considerable time and effort in treating a patient, he is likely to rate the outcome a success if only to justify himself and his labors. Nevertheless, allowing for a certain amount of error, it seems not unreasonable to accept the reported figures as a fair estimate. Despite possible fallacies, the ratings were made by trained clinicians and based on a great deal of information concerning the patient. The fact that numerous other studies have reported improvement rates of similar magnitude further strengthens their validity.

The control groups, according to Eysenck's contention, "recovered spontaneously" without any formal treatment. But what does "spontaneous recovery" mean? Essentially it means that the patient improved without the benefit of specific interventions or as a result of factors concerning which there is no information. Clinical experience, in the form of observations by trained psychotherapists over many years, does not bear out Eysenck's claim. Patients who are seriously disturbed typically do not "recover" from their neurotic problems although, with changes in their life situation and similar factors, acute symptoms often abate. This, however, does not mean that patients have learned to cope more adequately with their problems in living. Furthermore, Eysenck's study presents the paradoxical result of an inverse relationship between the intensity of the treatment effort and its outcome. That is, untreated patients showed the greatest improvement, patients treated by eclectic psychotherapy occupied a middle position, and those treated by psychoanalysis ranked lowest. While controlled studies sometimes emerge with findings that clash with accepted beliefs, in this case the results are so greatly at variance with observation and experience that the reader's credulity is sorely strained. (See Bergin's Comment, p. 95.)

If one examines the judgments of outcome one cannot escape the conclusion that mental hospitals and general practitioners used very different standards in making judgments of improvement. It is quite likely that almost any patient discharged from a state mental hospital after a period of time will obtain an official rating of "improved." In the case of the general practitioners one may also expect rather loose judgments. In both cases the amount of information supporting the ratings is bound to be less than in the case of experienced psychotherapists. While the comparability of the various ratings remains unknown, one is not justified in ignoring the lack of information, as was done by Eysenck.

As we have seen earlier in this chapter, definitions of outcome involve complex problems, almost all of which were disregarded in Eysenck's study. All the reader learns is that someone, using criteria of his own choosing, characterized the patient as improved. It follows that *in the absence of pertinent information, no meaningful comparisons can be carried out and no conclusions about the merit of any form of psychotherapy can be drawn. The most one can say is that the efficacy of psychotherapy is an open issue.*

3. *Absence of information concerning the therapeutic interaction.* While Eysenck did not dwell on this problem, he likened neurotic disorders to physical illness and psychotherapy to a form of medical treatment. Because of these assumptions Eysenck also spoke about "improvement" and "cure" in terms of restoring the patient to a previous state of health. It has been made clear throughout this volume that these suppositions are not tenable.

Moreover, psychotherapy was regarded as analogous to a pharmacological agent whose chemical composition was known. Beyond calling the forms of psychotherapy "psychoanalytic" or "eclectic," no specification was given concerning the *actual process of treatment,* including the nature of the patient's problems, the level of experience and attitudes of the therapists, and the precise nature of the interventions they employed. While global descriptions of this kind were quite common several decades ago—Eysenck could do no more than rely on published reports which provided no further data on this subject—it is now being realized that such global labels obscure more than they clarify and that comparisons of therapeutic approaches cannot be performed until accurate information is substituted for shorthand descriptions.

The following study goes some distance in remedying these deficiencies but, as we shall see, it suffers from several others.

Description. Singling out anxiety as a research focus, Paul was interested in examining the relative efficiency of therapeutic procedures derived respectively from "disease" and "learning" models in the treatment of public-speaking situations. Specifically, the study was designed to compare insight-oriented psychotherapy with modified systematic desensitization (see Chapters 2 and 4).

Measures included a sizable battery of self-report tests, autonomic indices of anxiety and physiological arousal, and a behavioral checklist of performance anxiety. The therapists were five experienced practitioners representing a mixture of the Freudian, neo-Freudian, and Rogerian orientation. They were paid for their services by the investigator. See Table 6–2 for an outline of the experimental procedure.

Three methods of treatment were employed: (1) *insight-oriented psychotherapy,* described as consisting of traditional interview procedures aimed at insight; (2) *modified systematic desensitization* based on the procedures advocated by Wolpe (1958), including progressive relaxation and desensitization to anxiety-provoking stimuli; and (3) *attention-placebo,* a procedure administered by the same therapists for the purpose of determining the extent of improvement from nonspecific treatment effects, such as expectation of relief, attention and interest on the part of the therapist, and "faith." Subjects (Ss) ingested a placebo pill, represented to them as a "fast-acting tranquilizer," and underwent a task described as "very stressful."

Two control groups were employed, a no-treatment classroom control, which followed the same procedures as the experimental groups except for the treatment itself, and a no-contact classroom control, which took the pretreatment and follow-up battery but otherwise did not participate in the investigation.

Subjects were undergraduate college students enrolled in a public-speaking course. A letter accompanying the pretreatment battery, which was administered to 710 students, stated that the study was designed to determine "which people benefit most from various types of psychological procedures used to treat anxieties." About half the population expressed a desire for treatment. After screening, subjects identified as highly anxious were assigned to the various groups. Each treatment group comprised 15 Ss, the control groups 29 and 22 re-

Table 6-2 *Schematic Presentation of Paul's Investigation*

PROCEDURES	Experimental groups			Control groups	
	INSIGHT-ORIENTED PSYCHOTHERAPY N-15	SYSTEMATIC DESENSITIZATION N-15	ATTENTION PLACEBO N-15	NON-TREATMENT CLASSROOM N-29	NO-CONTACT CLASSROOM N-22
Self-report tests and data forms	✓	✓	✓	✓	✓
Pretreatment test speech; repeat of selected tests; pulse rate; palmar sweat index	✓	✓	✓	✓	—
Interview and assignment to treatment	✓	✓	✓	—	—
Psychotherapy (different forms)	✓	✓	✓	✓ (Classroom only)	—
Posttreatment test speech; selected tests; pulse rate; palmar sweat index	✓	✓	✓	—	—
Follow-up battery: selected tests	✓	✓	✓	✓	✓

spectively. These individuals appeared to be good bets for psychotherapy in terms of motivation, degree of disturbance, intelligence, age, social class, etc.

Following a pretreatment test speech, which was preceded by the stress measures, Ss were given an interview. They then entered therapy with their respective therapists. Each S had five hours of individual therapy over a period of six weeks. Upon termination, they gave a posttreatment test speech, accompanied by the same measures.

It is noteworthy that, to control for therapist differences, the five therapists administered all forms of therapy. However, since they were not familiar with the desensitization treatment, they were given special training. It may be assumed that they felt more at home with the traditional procedures they ordinarily used in their therapeutic work.

The results based on extensive statistical analyses (only one of which is presented here) showed systematic desensitization to be consistently superior to the other methods (see Figure 6-2). No differences were found between the effects of insight-oriented psychotherapy and the nonspecific effects of the attention-placebo treatment, although both groups showed greater anxiety reduction than the no-treatment control groups. Follow-up studies showed that the therapeutic gains were maintained and that no symptom substitution had occurred. On the basis of his results Paul concluded that therapy based on a learning model is highly effective in alleviating anxiety of the kind he investigated and that other studies similarly show that therapy based on learning principles is superior to traditional forms of therapy based on psychodynamic concepts.

CRITICISM OF PAUL'S RESEARCH

The study is an example of a well-controlled investigation of psychotherapy and reveals careful attention to problems of measurement and control. It appears necessary, however, to raise questions concerning some of its major conclusions.

1. Were the patients "real" patients? As we have seen, this question is partly a definitional problem. Paul was certainly at liberty to define the term as he did; however, it may be argued that his Ss ac-

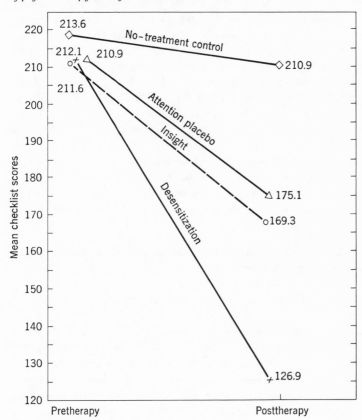

Fig. 6-2 *Changes in mean scores of observable manifestations of anxiety based on measures obtained at the beginning and at the end of psychotherapy (data from Paul, 1966).*

tually had little in common with persons who typically apply for psychotherapy to an outpatient clinic or a private practitioner. They were presumably well-functioning young adults who saw no need for psychotherapy prior to being approached by the investigator. True, the evidence showed that they experienced public-speaking anxiety, but it is questionable to what extent this constituted a serious problem in their lives. They did not see it as an incapacitating symptom for which they actively sought help.

There were other differences which distinguish these treatment conditions from more typical therapeutic situations: Whereas the bona fide neurotic patient must take the first step in enlisting professional help, the Ss in this study were *offered* psychotherapy. Little inconvenience or sacrifice in terms of money or time was involved, and they were spared the painful decision often faced by prospective patients of whether to admit defeat and seek help. There is little evidence that these students were suffering in any sense of the word. Besides being *invited* to participate, the professional services were provided as a courtesy. In sum, it appears that the students were more comparable to subjects participating in a psychological experiment than they were to patients seeking help for neurotic problems. In other words, while seemingly being a study of psychotherapy, it has only a resemblance to the process as it is usually understood. Studies of this kind are generally referred to as *analogue* research, some of which has been quite valuable. One of the major questions surrounding such investigations, however, concerns the extent to which findings obtained under simulated conditions can be generalized to actual therapy situations.[*]

2. Did the study provide a fair test of the relative merits of different forms of psychotherapy? In order to examine this question it is necessary to consider the goals of the two forms of therapy being compared. Insight-oriented psychotherapy was defined solely in terms of "traditional interview procedures" used by these therapists in their daily work. In this approach the therapist attempts to help the patient gain an emotional understanding (insight) of his problems, which in turn is expected to result in an alleviation of his anxiety symptoms. While the therapists asserted that "insight" was an important therapeutic goal in their work, there is no evidence that they focused specifically in the five hours allotted to them upon the reduction of the symptom defined as *public-speaking anxiety*. Evidently, they were given no instructions about the therapeutic goals as they had been de-

[*] Disagreeing with these observations, Paul (personal communication) states: "The Ss demonstrated both serious, central-life problems, with as severe anxiety reactions as appear in nearly any clinic, and more severe than most counseling bureaus—thus, I don't believe the *analogue* label is applicable." Regardless of the severity of their anxieties, the fact remains that the clients did not seek help on their own but instead were solicited to participate in the project. This appears to be a rather important distinction.

fined by the investigator nor was an effort made to insure uniformity of the therapeutic procedure. It is safe to infer that each therapist proceeded very differently, a problem which was not adequately solved by administering a checklist intended to assess the frequency with which they used a series of techniques *in general*. It appears that "traditional insight-oriented therapy" was inadequately defined and that the therapists were a rather heterogeneous group, as shown also by the mixture of theoretical orientations they professed.

While some therapists subscribing to a dynamic orientation specialize in brief or goal-limited psychotherapy, no evidence was presented that the therapists in this study typically worked along those lines. As we have seen in earlier chapters, dynamic therapists are not primarily concerned with the alleviation of an isolated symptom and they do not accept patients on that basis. Paul apparently induced them to work toward *his* goals rather than toward their own. Many therapists would have refused such an assignment.

As noted earlier, a specific symptom, as well as changes in a symptom, can be defined with far greater precision than changes in a person's self-concept, subjective comfort, competence in interpersonal relations, productivity, and sense of living up to one's potential. Available measuring instruments, like tests and rating scales, are for the most part inadequate for this kind of assessment. Does it follow that the changes desired by dynamic therapists do not occur? One possibility is that existing measuring instruments are insufficiently sensitive to register change. Thus, until adequate tools are developed, the issue must remain open.

The goals of psychotherapy and the form of therapy to be employed for reaching these goals obviously depend on the circumstances. If public-speaking anxiety is viewed as a specific symptom which one wishes to modify without regard for the broader context of the patient's total personality, behavior therapy may well be the treatment of choice. If on the other hand the symptom is seen only as a manifestation of a more pervasive disorder, the therapist (and the patient) may not be satisfied with an outcome which merely alleviates this particular symptom.

It may be argued that symptomatic changes may in turn generalize and the patient who has gained control over a troublesome problem may feel strengthened in other areas of his living as well. It is quite possible that in instances where the patient is not severely disturbed such an outcome is both economical and desirable. It is quite common these days for psychotherapists following divergent theoretical orientations to employ desensitization and other behavioral techniques as part of the total therapeutic effort.

What Paul's study has shown is that, given the circumstances he contrived, desensitization appears to work quite well, and numerous other studies support his findings. He is entitled to conclude that, under the stated conditions (and presumably similar ones), this form of psychotherapy—for which he clearly shows a preference—is helpful. What he has failed to do, as we have attempted to show, is (1) to study dynamic psychotherapy as it is commonly practiced, instead of which he devised a form of brief psychotherapy arbitrarily defined as *insight therapy;* and (2) to demonstrate the superiority of therapies based on a learning model to those based on dynamic conceptions. Paul's conclusions are not justified largely because the comparisons he performed are not the proper ones to make. If Paul's findings are restricted to the conditions of his experiment, they may be accepted. One should be extremely wary, however, in generalizing the conclusions, as Paul and others citing his work have done. For the indicated reasons, there are as yet no adequate comparisons of the type intended by Paul. Consequently, there is no reliable evidence of the superiority of one therapeutic approach over another, and even less of the effectiveness of psychotherapy compared to no treatment.

In the following chapter we shall examine some of the research topics mentioned above in greater detail and provide further illustrations.

Summary

The task of research in psychotherapy is to document insights gained by psychotherapists in the course of their clinical work, to test hypotheses generated by clinicians and theoreticians, and to shed light on the mechanisms involved in psychological change. The need for controlled investigative efforts in this area has been increasingly appreciated in recent years.

In order to assess quantitative and qualitative changes resulting from psychotherapy it is necessary to have precise measures of the patient's state before entering therapy, upon termination, and at followup. Furthermore, one must control intercurrent events in the patient's life so that observed changes can be reasonably attributed to the patient-therapist interaction (the independent variable). In addition, it is incumbent upon the researcher to provide accurate data about the nature of the therapeutic influence—the therapist's techniques in conjunction with personal attributes. Because of the complexity of these variables it has proven extraordinarily difficult to design and execute studies which satisfy scientific criteria. Most outcome studies are deficient in numerous respects, and comparisons of different forms of psychotherapy are distinctly premature. Reasons for the difficulties have been presented and two typical studies have been examined in some detail.

Suggested Readings

BERGIN, A. E., & GARFIELD, S. (Eds.) *Handbook of psychotherapy and behavior change: An empirical analysis.* New York: Wiley, 1970.

GOLDSTEIN, A. P., & DEAN, S. J. (Eds.) *The investigation of psychotherapy: Commentaries and readings.* New York: Wiley, 1966.

GOLDSTEIN, A. P., HELLER, K., & SECHREST, L. B. *Psychotherapy and the psychology of behavior change.* New York: Wiley, 1966.

GOTTSCHALK, L. A., & AUERBACH, A. H. (Eds.) *Research methods in psychotherapy.* New York: Appleton-Century-Crofts, 1966.

KIESLER, D. J. Some myths of psychotherapy research and the search for a paradigm. *Psychological Bulletin,* 1966, **65**, 110–136.

ROGERS, C. R., & DYMOND, R. F. *Psychotherapy and personality change.* Chicago: University of Chicago, 1954.

RUBINSTEIN, E. A., & PARLOFF, M. B. (Eds.) *Research in psychotherapy.* Washington, D. C.: American Psychological Association, 1959.

SHLIEN, J. M., HUNT, H. F., MATARAZZO, J. D., & SAVAGE, C. *Research in psychotherapy.* Vol. 3. Washington, D. C.: American Psychological Association, 1968.

STRUPP, H. H. The outcome problem in psychotherapy revisited. *Psychotherapy*, 1963, **1**, 1–13.

STRUPP, H. H., & LUBORSKY, L. (Eds.) *Research in psychotherapy.* Vol. 2. Washington, D. C.: American Psychological Association, 1962.

TRUAX, C. B., & CARKHUFF, R. R. *Toward effective counseling and psychotherapy: Training and practice.* Chicago: Aldine, 1967.

CHAPTER 7

A CLOSER LOOK AT
RESEARCH ON PATIENTS,
THERAPISTS, AND TECHNIQUES

The Quest for Specificity

In the preceding chapter we have discussed some of the basic problems of research in psychotherapy, with major focus on the evaluations of therapeutic outcomes. We have also noted that major factors determining success or failure in a given case are attributable to (1) the therapist, (2) the patient, and (3) the transactions occurring between patient and therapist. To these must be added (4) situational factors, both within therapy and external to it, which affect the foregoing variables. During the past two or three decades a considerable amount of research has been devoted to the task of clarifying these problems. A recent bibliography (Strupp & Bergin, 1969), confined to individual psychotherapy with adult patients, lists some 2,700 references.

Despite these vigorous efforts, research in psychotherapy has not exerted a deep influence on therapeutic *practice*. Partly this is due to the fact that the results of most investigations have not had substantial practical significance. Furthermore, we must consider the relatively short period of time systematic research has been in existence, deficiencies in research techniques, and practical difficulties in designing and carrying out adequately controlled studies.

Typical problems facing the researcher have already been mentioned. As we have noted, researchers are faced with serious limitations in collecting and analyzing data from representative samples of patients and therapists; follow-up studies have been difficult to carry out; the crucial requirement of enlisting the full cooperation of therapists, patients, and institutions has been a continual stumbling block; and, in general, rigorous designs have been difficult to impose upon the therapeutic phenomena themselves. Finally, researchers who have attacked problems in the area through experimental simulations (analogues) have not succeeded in relating their findings to actual therapy situations.

As research has progressed it has become increasingly clear that *psychotherapy as currently practiced is not a unitary process and is not applied to a unitary problem. Consequently, the traditional question, "Is psychotherapy effective?" is no longer fruitful or appropriate.*

In light of these considerations, the question of the goal of psychotherapy research in its most general terms should be reformulated as follows: *What specific therapeutic interventions produce specific changes in specific patients under specific conditions?* In order to answer this ultimate question, it is essential to break it down into manageable components and direct research to each subarea. In other words, we must achieve greater specificity concerning all elements of the psychotherapeutic process. Consider the following statement by an eminent clinician which illustrates the point:

> In my early years as an analyst I was taught the idea that any well-trained analyst could do a good job on any analyzable patient . . . I now believe that one analyst can sometimes take a particular patient further than another because his temperament and life experience fit him to understand this type of patient especially well [Thompson, 1956, p. 534].

As a generalization by an experienced therapist this statement is undoubtedly valuable, but can it help other therapists to make more judicious choices in selecting their patients? Does it tell a therapist how he might work more effectively toward particular therapeutic goals? What are these goals? What patient characteristics are conducive to a better therapeutic outcome? How can one maximize the chances that a particular patient in interaction with a particular therapist will be successful? What constitutes an experienced therapist? What kind of training and supervision should he have to become a competent practitioner? What are the prerequisites in terms of personality and attitudes which enable the therapist to do an effective job? These are some of the questions which research must seek to answer so that therapeutic techniques may become more precise, focused, and efficient.

Some of the important implications of Thompson's statement may be stated as follows:

1. Contrary to earlier assumptions, *therapists* can no longer be regarded as interchangeable units who administer a clearly definable treatment, even if they subscribe to similar theoretical assumptions and their training has been highly comparable. Instead, we are forced to realize that different therapists, depending on variables in their personality, training, experience, outlook on life, and personal values, exert different effects on a patient regardless of the particular therapeutic techniques they may employ.

2. Similarly, *patients*, depending on variables in their personality, intelligence, education, socioeconomic status, cultural background, and—last but by no means least—the nature of their emotional problems (traditionally termed "psychopathology"), are differentially receptive to different forms of therapeutic influence. In other words, we must endeavor to transcend such broad designations as *hysteric, phobic, obsessive-compulsive* by more precise descriptions of emotional problems and their amenability to psychotherapy.

3. *Technique* variables cannot be dealt with in isolation but must be viewed in the context of patient and therapist variables enumerated above. For example, a form of psychotherapy is defined only in the broadest terms if it is called *psychoanalysis, client-centered therapy* or *behavior therapy,* and these labels may in fact obscure the essential ingredients of the psychotherapeutic influence which themselves are in need of definition, isolation, and measurement. Furthermore, we must be mindful of the fact that techniques are not administered in a vacuum but are almost an integral part of the therapist who practices them. Consequently, any technique is inevitably influenced—and perhaps markedly modified—by the personality characteristics of the therapist.

Although the specification of these variables is unquestionably important, the researcher realizes that no variable exists in isolation. Variables in the therapist interact with each other, as do variables within the patient. Finally, patient, therapist, and technique variables influence each other in complex ways and are in turn modified by situational factors. This is one important reason for the assertion that the assessment of therapeutic outcomes must remain a hazardous undertaking until greater clarification of salient variables and their interaction is achieved. To be sure, science always follows a process of approximation, and in psychotherapy it may never be possible to bring even the majority of important variables under experimental control. This discussion, therefore, is only schematic, and it describes an ideal which we can at best hope to approach as investigative efforts proceed.

In the remainder of this chapter we shall take a somewhat closer look at the major subareas and cite the results of some typical research.

The Therapist as a Variable in Psychotherapy

As modern psychotherapy began to evolve at the end of the nineteenth century, major emphasis was placed on the refinement of techniques for bringing about therapeutic change. As we have seen, Freud defined the role of the therapist as that of a relatively passive observer who paid "evenly hovering" attention to the patient's verbal and nonverbal communications, including their symbolic meanings, and confined his activity (at least, ideally) to interpretations designed to overcome resistances and correct the patient's faulty beliefs. He admitted that at times the therapist had to serve the patient as a model and mentor but, in keeping with his efforts to set psychoanalysis apart from other forms of psychotherapy which employed suggestion, persuasion, and exhortation, he sought to minimize the therapist's personal influence. Instead he regarded the therapist as a technician who consistently encouraged the patient's self-expression and confined his interventions to well-timed interpretations. Thus it was expected that the patient would gain increasing strength to face and master his conflicts and eventually become a self-reliant and independent adult. From these conceptualizations it also followed that one person who had received thorough training in analytic doctrine and analytic techniques was largely equivalent to another person who had undergone similar training. Therefore, it was assumed that despite personal idiosyncrasies all analytic therapists proceeded very similarly and the nature of their therapeutic influence was essentially identical. The role of the psychotherapist was to be no different from that of a surgeon who applies a well-defined operative procedure and whose personality is of little consequence.

Freud (1910) soon realized, however, that the situation was considerably more complicated. In particular, he noted that not infrequently the therapist's clinical observations, as well as his judgment and techniques, were adversely affected by his own emotional reactions to the patient, notably at those times when the patient dealt with conflicts which the therapist had not resolved himself. As a consequence, the therapist might subtly steer the patient away from such material, give excessive reassurance, respond with anger, and in other respects render him a disservice. These untoward reactions, which Freud regarded as potentially serious interferences with the progress of therapy, especially if the therapist were unaware of their occurrence, were termed *countertransference*. Largely to counteract these tendencies but also to provide the therapist with a deeper understanding of his own unconscious processes and defense mechanisms, Freud insisted that every therapist as part of his training should undergo a so-called didactic or training analysis, in the course of which he would become aware of his own emotional blind spots, thereby eliminating the pitfalls of countertransference reactions. Freud never believed that a training analysis could completely obviate countertransference, but he regarded it as the best course of action for increasing the therapist's objectivity and effectiveness. A training analysis, now largely indistinguishable from a therapeutic analysis, has become an integral part of psychoanalytic training, and other forms of therapy (for example, client-centered therapy) have similarly recognized the pedagogic value of placing the trainee in the patient role. In more general terms, the significance of Freud's recommendation is to be found in the realization that the clinical observer, more than the physical scientist, is prone to make faulty observations because his perception and judgment are susceptible to influence by the phenomena he wishes to observe. The training analysis may thus be likened to a process of calibrating a scientific instrument.

While Freud keenly appreciated the potential interferences stemming from the therapist's personality, he paid less attention to positive attributes of the personality which might heighten the therapeutic influence. Of course, he acknowledged the importance of tact, respect for the patient, uncompromising honesty, etc., and demanded that the therapist should have "a comparatively high degree of psychical normality and correct adjustment" (Freud, 1937), but he saw these attributes as subordinate to the therapist's technical skills. In more recent years the therapist's personality has come under closer scrutiny, and a substantial amount of research has been focused upon it. Some of it has been conducted within the analytic framework, but more significant contributions have come from workers within client-centered therapy, which elevated the therapist's attitude (see Chapter 3) to a position of preeminence in psychotherapy. Indeed, many workers today regard *the therapist's personality and the attitudes he brings to bear upon the treatment situation as the key to the thera-*

peutic influence, and perhaps of greater importance than any technique he might employ.

General personality characteristics. Holt and Luborsky (1958), working at the Menninger Foundation, one of the major training and treatment centers in the country, evaluated psychiatric residents on a large number of personality traits by means of personality tests and clinical assessments at various stages of their training. They succeeded in isolating three sets of variables considered desirable in a psychotherapist: (1) genuineness (versus facade); (2) social adjustment with co-workers; and (3) freedom from status-mindedness. In addition, self-objectivity (akin to self-understanding), mature heterosexual adjustment, and adequate emotional control were mentioned as important attributes. Krasner (1963) listed several dozen laudatory characteristics which the "ideal" therapist, according to various authors, is supposed to possess. No human being obviously can be such a paragon of virtues. Therefore, it is questionable whether the concept of the "ideal therapist" has much practical meaning. Nor do *general* personality variables seem to have much bearing on the quality of the therapeutic relationship (Gardner, 1964). Studies in which therapist personality characteristics were measured in the context of the therapeutic interaction, as will be seen, have shown greater promise.

Warmth, acceptance, empathy. Warmth, acceptance, empathy, effort to understand, spontaneity, and related variables have been studied extensively since Rogers' original formulations (Raush & Bordin, 1957; Truax & Carkhuff, 1967). Truax's Accurate Empathy Scale has emerged as one of the best measures of these variables. Truax defines accurate empathy as "sensitivity to current feelings and the verbal facility to communicate this understanding in a language attuned to the client's current being." Empathy is judged by two or more raters directly from tape recordings. This and other measures of empathy have been utilized in numerous studies, all of which demonstrate a positive correlation between therapist empathy, patient self-exploration, and independent criteria of patient change.

Another important finding (Truax & Carkhuff, 1967) is that empathy, warmth, etc. are created by the therapist and are largely independent of patient characteristics. These authors also conclude that therapist variables, besides those investigated by them, may contribute equally to therapeutic outcomes. In the light of these findings, empathy, acceptance, and warmth are best viewed as necessary but not sufficient conditions. In general, the evidence supports the view that some therapists are more effective than others—they seem to have greater "penetrance"—and one essential difference may lie along one of the foregoing dimensions.

Therapists' values. It seems reasonable to assume that in the course of successful therapy the patient assimilates some of the therapist's social and cultural values, his attitudes toward mental health and illness, his judgments about the patient's wishes, impulses, aspirations, actions, and so forth. Although a therapist may try to refrain from communicating his personal values, it is quite likely that over a period of time the patient may nevertheless be able to ferret them out. The extent to which the therapist refrains from communicating his values is of course partly a function of his theoretical predilections; at one extreme he may strenuously avoid communicating his values, perhaps on the grounds that he might perpetuate the patient's need for guidance from others; at the other extreme, he may feel that it is highly desirable for the patient to supplant his own prejudices with what one would hope are the therapist's more accepting, tolerant, and enlightened views. However, the therapist, being a member of the same culture and usually of the same social class as the patient, may communicate these values regardless of his conscious intention. One investigator (Rosenthal, 1955) showed that patients who improved in therapy tended to revise certain of their moral values in the direction of the therapist's values. More recent research (e.g., Buhler, 1962; Welkowitz, Cohen, & Ortmeyer, 1967) tends to support these results. The research by Bandura and his group (Bandura, 1965) clearly suggests that in various respects the therapist serves as a model whose behavior is imitated by the patient. However, much work needs to be done to explore the problem in greater depth.

Interest and liking. The hypothesis that the therapist's interest and liking may be a therapeutic factor has produced contradictory evidence (McNair, Lorr, & Callahan, 1963; Stoler, 1963; Waskow, 1963). However, it seems safe to predict that therapists who actively dislike certain patients will not work well with them (Strupp, 1960; Strupp & Williams, 1960).

Countertransference. While research on this problem has proved difficult, the evidence (Bandura, 1956; Bandura, Lipsher, & Miller, 1960; Cutler, 1958) generally suggests that therapist conflicts in relation to hostility, dependency, warmth, and intimacy have an adverse effect upon the patient's performance in therapy.

Therapist experience level. Experience is not strictly a personality variable, nor has it been possible so far to study systematically the effects of the therapist's experience on outcome. Apart from the fact that experience is a broad term (including training, maturation, personal therapy), sizable samples of experienced therapists have not been available to researchers. Indeed, many findings in the entire area are based on the performance of neophytes who often fail to merit the appellation "psychotherapist." Investigations bearing on this variable not unexpectedly favor experienced therapists (Ashby, Ford, Guerney, & Guerney, 1957; Bohn, 1965; Cartwright & Vogel, 1960; Fiedler, 1950a, 1950b; Rice, 1965; Strupp, 1955), but it remains to be demonstrated how experience heightens therapeutic competence.

Theoretical orientation. Relationships between the therapist's theoretical orientation and his practices have been demonstrated in a number of studies (Strupp, 1962), but we know as yet little about the importance of these associations in relation to therapeutic outcomes.

DOES THERAPIST "TYPE" INFLUENCE PATIENT RESPONSE TO PSYCHOTHERAPY?: AN ILLUSTRATIVE STUDY

In several articles, Whitehorn and Betz (1954, 1960) presented evidence that psychotherapists who were highly successful with hospitalized schizophrenic patients (type A) differed from therapists who had lower improvement rates with such patients. Type A therapists, according to these studies, were more successful because they were able to place technical considerations in the service of a truly collaborative therapeutic relationship and this in turn produced more favorable therapeutic results. The data were obtained largely from clinic notes and hospital records which were studied by these investigators after completion of the treatment. Subsequently it was found that there were differences in the interest patterns of A and B therapists, as measured by the Strong Vocational Interest Blank, one of the widely used tests of vocational interests. Specifically, it was possible to select a group of twenty-three items (subsequently called the A-B scale) which sharply differentiated the two types of therapists. Type A therapists scored high on interest patterns characterizing lawyers and certified public accountants but low on the keys for printer and mathematics-physical science teacher. Subsequent research corroborated the stability of this measure.

One of the important problems raised by this work related to the question of whether the findings were confined to schizophrenic patients or if they might also hold true for nonhospitalized neurotic patients. Therefore, McNair, Callahan, and Lorr (1962) tested the hypothesis that therapists typed as A and therapists typed as B are not equally effective with neurotic outpatients in psychotherapy.

They administered the Strong to fifty-five male therapists in seven outpatient clinics of the Veterans Administration and selected twenty therapists with the highest and twenty therapists with the lowest scores on the A-B scale. The therapists did not differ in terms of experience or competence, as rated by clinical psychologists. Most therapists adhered to a Freudian or an eclectic orientation.

The patients in this study were forty male outpatients, each of whom was treated by one of the above therapists. Patients seen by A or B therapists did not differ significantly in terms of age (mean age was about thirty-five years) or education (both groups typically had some college education), and the groups included an equal number of unemployed patients. Both groups were seen in weekly interviews over a period of four months, which is fairly common for outpatient clinics. Patients took a series of psychological tests and underwent the usual clinic diagnostic tests prior to and following the treatment. In addition, there were assessments by the therapists and by social workers, and a follow-up was conducted one year after treatment started.

The results of the statistical analysis indicated that patients treated by B therapists improved significantly more than patients of A therapists. After one year, patients of B therapists still continued to show greater improvement. Thus, the results were the opposite of those obtained by Whitehorn and Betz on schizophrenic patients.

In searching for explanations of their findings the authors examined various possibilities without coming to definite conclusions. Conceivably, type B therapists had interests more in common with their patients than type A therapists, which might also be the basis for the earlier results. However, there were no indications that A and B therapists reacted differently to their patients.

Since the publication of the work by Whitehorn and Betz, a considerable amount of research has been devoted to the A-B distinction. While the latter has been described as "a very useful organizing framework for exploring important process-outcome relationships in the psychological treatment of behavior disorders" (Carson, 1967), the distinction is primarily an empirical one, and there is no good theory to account for the observed differences among therapists.

The foregoing study is a representative example of research dealing with therapist "types." While it may be possible to place therapists in certain broad categories, of which the A-B typology is a good example, many other variables are at work in any given patient-therapist relationship, and therapist type may play only a small part in therapeutic outcomes.

RÉSUMÉ

From everything we know, there can be little doubt that the person of the therapist represents an important force, both in a positive and negative sense, in the therapeutic encounter. Client-centered therapists have placed personal qualities of the therapist on a pedestal, whereas psychoanalysts and behavior therapists have accorded them relatively scant attention. The route by which therapist personality factors enter and influence techniques, however, needs to be mapped out much more thoroughly, and at present it is not at all clear how therapist personality and technical operations are to be differentiated.

Prominently researched personality dispositions of the therapist include such variables as empathy, warmth, and genuineness, and measurement of these variables has met with fair success. Contrary to earlier contentions, however, they can not be regarded as the sole, or even the major, factor determining therapeutic outcome. It seems more reasonable to conclude that once the therapist has achieved a fair level of therapeutic skill and is successful in providing a modicum of warmth, empathy, etc., outcome is more importantly a function of technical competence and patient characteristics.

The Patient as a Variable in Psychotherapy

The roots of modern psychotherapy, as we have repeatedly noted, are found in the medical tradition, and the conditions for which psychotherapy seemed indicated were viewed as analogous to diseases. In order to treat a disease effectively it is necessary to make an accurate diagnosis—that is, to identify the disease entity (syndrome)—and then to institute a course of action (treatment) in order to correct or counteract the malfunction. This ideal cannot always be realized, but in general it may be said that in medicine effective treatment is dependent upon accurate diagnosis as well as the amount of information available concerning the underlying causes of the manifestations (symptoms). For example, the physician can from a set of symptoms diagnose an inflamed appendix and will usually choose surgical removal as the treatment. Furthermore, this is a radical treatment in the sense that it removes the cause of the underlying difficulty and restores the patient to health.

It was logical, therefore, for Breuer and Freud, who worked in the medical tradition, to search for a method of treatment that might help patients suffering from hysteria, which was viewed as disease. In our time, some authors (e.g., Szasz, 1961) have disputed that hysteria is a disease in the medical sense. Its symptomatology is certainly highly diffuse. Nevertheless, it is possible to distinguish personality types who may either manifest hysterical symptoms or who have the propensity to develop them under stressful circumstances. Similarly, one may define other types, for example, obsessive-compulsive, phobic, which, at least in a broad sense, serve to classify individuals. The study of psychological malfunctions falls to the field of *psychopathology*, and the classification of mental disturbances is the province of *nosology*. It is sufficient to mention in this context that the major classification system in use today is the one set forth in the *Diagnostic and Statistical Manual of the American Psychiatric Association.*

The method of treatment developed by Freud and his followers was considered maximally useful for the so-called transference neuroses, which included hysteria, phobic conditions, and obsessive-compulsive neuroses. By contrast, patients who were unable to develop a transference relationship in therapy (cf. Chapter 2), such as psychopaths (individuals who engage in antisocial behavior without experiencing a significant amount of guilt or anxiety) and schizophrenics (persons suffering from a major psychosis), were judged to be largely unsuitable for psychoanalysis.

The point to be made is that in his early work Freud endeavored to find a specific form of psychotherapy for a specific condition and he laid down a number of criteria for evaluating the suitability of prospective patients for psychoanalysis (prognosis). Among the prerequisites were youth, a fairly high level of intelligence, education, a certain emotional maturity, and the ability to introspect and take some distance from one's feelings and emotional reactions. A form of therapy cannot be faulted if it is effective only under some conditions, and panaceas are hardly to be expected. However, as time went on, the scope of psychoanalysis (as well as other forms of psychotherapy) gradually increased and stringent discriminations concerning its applicability tended to become blurred. Commenting on these developments, Anna Freud (1954) speculates that more systematic efforts to refine therapy aimed at the transference neuroses would have been far more fruitful.

In recent years, partly as a function of the efforts by behaviorally oriented therapists, there has been a revival of interest in the search for specific treatments for specific conditions. Strupp and Bergin (1969) formulated the problem in these terms: "Which patient characteristics and problems are most amenable to which techniques conducted by which type of therapist in what type of setting?" They noted further:

> Thus, rather than the more common approach of trying to determine the type of patient or initial status which will respond best to a nebulous and heterogeneous definition of psychotherapy, it is more important to devise specific therapies that will change particular kinds of patients or problems. While it may seem totally obvious that differential initial sta-

tus should be paired with differential treatment, there is hardly a program of research in existence which deals systematically with this problem.

At present there is no evidence that different types of patients are differentially responsive to psychoanalytic, client-centered, or other forms of psychotherapy. This does not mean that such differences do not exist, but for the reasons discussed in the preceding chapter it has been impossible to study homogeneous patient groups in relation to homogeneous therapeutic techniques. On the other hand, when therapists have attempted to modify specific behaviors or focal symptoms by means of behavioral techniques (cf. Chapter 4) the results have been more encouraging. Nevertheless, in interpreting these findings it is well to keep in mind the strictures discussed in the context of the Paul (1966) study (cf. Chapter 6), particularly the observation that criteria which measure the more subtle and complex affective and cognitive types of changes reveal no significant differences between behavioral and other procedures. This point is further illustrated by reference to a British study (Gelder, Marks, & Wolff, 1967).

These authors studied patients whose presenting symptoms included a main phobia, subsidiary phobias, anxiety, and depression. They found that desensitization was more effective in decreasing phobic responses of a specific or focal type, such as reported by Paul; however, the differences between treatments disappeared when patients with more complex symptoms or more severe anxiety were studied or when criteria measuring anxiety and depression were used as outcome indices. While this research was based upon work by inexperienced psychiatric residents and is open to criticism on other grounds, it is illustrative of a direction of movement in research and treatment which may be of great potential significance.

It is becoming increasingly clear that patients cannot be categorized very effectively in terms of the traditional labels mentioned previously. Instead new dimensions must be found which bear a closer relationship to expectable treatment outcomes. Examples of such dimensions will be briefly mentioned:

Openness to therapeutic influences. It has been recognized that some patients are more open to therapeutic influence than others. Several lines of investigation suggest that the patient's willingness to deal with his problems (motivation for therapy) and his ability to express and communicate his feelings are predictors of positive movement in psychotherapy. The best measures of these characteristics have been derived from patient verbal behavior during initial interviews (White, Fichtenbaum, & Dollard, 1964; Truax & Carkhuff, 1967; Rogers et al., 1967). The measures include: willingness to express feelings (versus resistance), liking for the therapist and the therapy process, having and experiencing strong dependency needs, experiencing guilt and anxiety, sensing personal responsibility for problems, wanting help, willingness to see disorder in psychological instead of medical terms, attending to internal events, etc. An advantage of these measures derives from the fact that they are based on actual in-therapy behavior; that is, they are firmly supported by empirical data. In practical terms, the best way to determine a patient's suitability for therapy may be to accept him provisionally for psychotherapy and to observe his behavior in the therapy situation.

Patient attractiveness. While the therapist's technical expertise is important, it is equally clear that his personal reactions to the patient may influence the course and outcome of therapy (Strupp, 1960). A number of the variables noted above obtain their significance not only by their relationship to the effects of particular techniques but also by the fact that they determine how the therapist as a person responds to them. For example, studies by Nash, Hoehn-Saric, Battle, Stone, Imber, and Frank (1965) and Heller and Goldstein (1961) reported outcomes favoring the more attractive patients. The measures used in these studies are similar to rating scales which evaluate patient likability, a variable which has yielded contradictory results, but which generally indicates a more favorable prognosis for the more likable patients (Strupp & Williams, 1960). No studies have as yet separated the qualities and effects of such attractiveness measures from the motivational and behavioral qualities described under "openness to therapeutic influence," so it is presently unclear whether these sets of measures are interdependent and, if so, to what extent.

Patient "relatability." In addition to facilitating engagement in the process of self-evaluation and change, the preceding variables probably determine the degree to which a relationship is formed between therapist and patient. To the extent that the relationship itself is a therapeutic agent, this factor becomes crucial. Isaacs & Haggard's (1966) measure of "relatability," derived from the Thematic Apperception Test, a widely used projective technique, found striking differences in outcomes of patients rated high and low in this quality. Presumably, the differentiating power of this variable as well as the preceding ones could be enhanced by more carefully pairing patient and therapist in order to heighten the openness, attractiveness, and relatability of the patient (and possibly vice versa).

Congruence in patient's and therapist's expectations. This variable has been shown to be consistently related to the psychotherapy process (Lennard & Bernstein, 1960). Heine and Trosman (1960) and Overall and Aronson (1963) have also found that congruence between the patient's and therapist's expectations from psychotherapy is positively related to continuation in therapy. Clemes and D'Andrea (1965) reported that patients who received an interview from a psychiatric resident compatible with their expectations were significantly less anxious than those who had an interview that conflicted with their expectations. Not surprisingly, therapists indicated that the latter kind of interview was more difficult to conduct. Furthermore, patients having expectations congruent with those of therapists remained longer in therapy. Two main types of patient expectation have been noted in this area of research by Heine and Trosman: (1) *guidance expectation*, or the expectancy of receiving advice and being told what to do; and (2) *participation expectation*, an expectancy of taking an active role in the attempt to arrive at a solution to one's problems. Accordingly, a patient is helped more when he receives therapy which is consistent with his expectations (Goin, Yamamoto, & Silverman, 1965; Levitt, 1966). While congruence of patient and therapist expectations clearly has a favorable effect upon the process and duration of therapy, it would be of value to learn in greater detail how congruence or discrepancy in expectation influences outcome. The above studies have more or less uniformly assumed that therapists are homogeneous with respect to the expectations they have of the therapy relationship and that it is the patients who have varying expectations. This may not be a tenable assumption since therapists may also diverge in their expectations.

Socioeconomic class. The importance of the patient's socioeconomic class as a variable in psychotherapy has been stressed by numerous authors (e.g., Hollingshead & Redlich, 1958; Strupp & Williams, 1960; Auld & Myers, 1954).

The variable of *similarity* in socioeconomic class between patient and therapist may become even more relevant in view of the trend towards greater utilization of lay therapists who could be of lower socioeconomic class. Several studies have indicated that therapists of lower socioeconomic class or educational level are as effective or more effective with lower class patients than professionals (Poser, 1966; Deane & Ansbacher, 1962; Lohrenz, Hunter, & Schwartzman, 1966; Carkhuff & Truax, 1965). The results of one study (Keith-Spiegel & Spiegel, 1967) are especially interesting in this regard. The researchers found that the higher the educational level of the patient, the more psychiatrists and psychologists were viewed as most helpful, and the lower the educational level of the patient, the more help was seen as having been given by aides and fellow patients. One male patient with a reported IQ of 83 was quoted as saying, "My doctor was a nice enough guy but I never knew what the hell he was talking about. He didn't make no sense at all. Only time I felt better was when me and the boys would knock around our problems while playing pool" [Cartwright, 1968, p. 397].

It appears that characteristics of the therapeutic relationship, as they may be determined by patient variables we have been discussing, markedly influence the quality and timing of susceptibility to influence and change. Relationship factors, therefore, may be seen as a prerequisite for therapeutic influence rather than as an end in themselves, and they may be regarded as the matrix within which planful interventions can occur. Therefore, therapist personality characteristics in conjunction with patient characteristics under optimal conditions interact to produce a readiness to be influenced in the patient, and part of the therapist's skill is demonstrated by creating this condition and recognizing its existence, at which times he can employ technical maneuvers to therapeutic ends. *It is the manner in which the therapist uses and perhaps exploits this condition, whenever it exists at varying times in therapy, that constitutes his effectiveness as a professional influencer, reinforcer, desensitizer, model, or whatever term one chooses.*

Degree of disturbance. Several studies suggest that patients who are better adjusted at the beginning of therapy show the greatest improvement while the more severely disturbed patients show the least improvement (Gelder, Marks, & Wolff, 1967; Stone, Frank, Nash, & Imber, 1961; Stephens & Astrup, 1965). This is consonant with Luborsky's wry summary: "Those who stay in treatment improve; those who improve are better off to begin with than those who do not; and one can predict response to treatment by how well they are to begin with" [1959, p. 324].

A refinement of this formulation has been provided by Truax and Carkhuff (1967) who state: *"the greater the initial psychological disturbance* (measured by self-report psychological test, etc.) but *the lesser the initial behavioral disturbance* (measured by prior length of institutionalization, etc.) the greater the predicted improvement" [pp. 170–172]. This statement emphasizes the point that those patients who, while struggling with severe psychological conflicts, still manage to meet life's responsibilities are the better therapeutic risks. Further implications of this statement may be that the better risk patients are more anxious but still coping, have greater ego strength (as demonstrated by their continuing struggle against inner conflicts), and for these reasons are more highly motivated to enter therapy, stay in therapy once they are accepted, and see it through (Strupp, Fox, & Lessler, 1969).

Adapting techniques to fit the patient. Psychotherapists face the decision of selecting patients to fit their preferred techniques or making the techniques more suitable for a wider range of patients. Psychoanalysis has typically followed the first course, whereas today greater efforts are being made to tailor therapeutic techniques to patient characteristics.

Attempts to directly modify traditional approaches have focused upon the use of information, instruction, and modeling as techniques for overcoming inability or resistance to employing therapy in an efficient way. For instance, Hoehn-Saric, Frank, Imber, Nash, Stone, and Battle (1964) demonstrated that a role induction technique which involved all three of these procedures had a favorable effect on therapeutic outcomes with clinic patients. Truax and Carkhuff (1965) successfully utilized a tape recording of "good therapy behavior" which they presented to prospective clients, and Goldstein, Heller, and Sechrest (1966) suggest the use of films for similar purposes.

Other workers have found that highly anxious subjects respond best to focused interviews, whereas less anxious subjects respond best to free association interviews (Kaplan, 1966; Sifneos, 1967); lower class subjects who are given concrete advice improve more than those who do not receive it (Goin, Yamamoto, & Silverman, 1965); blue-collar workers respond better when the therapist is more informal, flexible, directive, physically active, concrete, and willing to meet outside of the consulting room (Gould, 1967); more open and mature, accepting and flexible therapists are able to modify their approaches to meet the needs of less "appropriate" clients and thus are more successful in keeping more of them in treatment (84 percent) (Baum, Felzer, D'Zmura, & Shumaker, 1966); a job-oriented, concrete, flexible, individually tailored program incorporating intensiveness of contact and remedial education is successful in helping delinquent boys (Massimo & Shore, 1963).

In sum, recognizing the deficiencies of traditional diagnostic labels, it is important to define the complexity of initial patient status with sufficient rigor so that one can determine whether a given technique is modifying only part or all of the patient's symptomatology. Thus, while it may be important to know that phobias are responsive to desensitization, it is equally important to know what is happening to the rest of the patient's experience and life. Diagnostic evaluations of prospective patients should result in assessments concerning (1) the degree and quality of changes that may be expected as a result of therapeutic intervention; (2) the kind of therapy from which the patient is likely to benefit (as well as methods that may be less suitable for him); and (3) the kinds of therapist characteristics to which the patient may be expected to respond most favorably.

As we have noted, there may be large groups of patients who are unsuitable for almost all forms of treatment because of such variables as poor intelligence, lack of motivation for active participation required in traditional forms of psychotherapy, severity and chronicity of disturbance, deeply ingrained characterological deficits, poor ability to introspect and verbalize feelings, and the like. Psychotherapy (including behavior therapy) may not be the treatment of choice for all applicants, and it is no more than realistic to face this likely possibility. In exceptional cases it may still be desirable to accept a patient for therapy whose prognosis is poor, but in that event the chances for improvement must be weighed against the expenditure of time, effort, expense, and the like. Such judgments, of course, have long been made informally by clinicians, but there exists a great need to empirically formalize them.

If it turns out that only a minority of disturbed persons is suitable for or amenable to psychotherapy as it is currently practiced, greater effort must be made to modify existing techniques to meet the needs of these various subclasses of patients.

Finally, it has become evident that patient variables, while conceptually distinct, must properly be discussed in terms of *interaction* with therapist variables, and this, as we shall see, is equally true of technique variables.

Technique in Psychotherapy

Technique in psychotherapy refers to the technical operations by means of which one person (therapist) deliberately influences the feelings, emotions, attitudes, beliefs, and actions of another (patient). The therapist therefore may be viewed as a professional whose influence is in many ways comparable to that of a parent, educator, priest, propagandist, politician, and the like (Frank, 1961). Granted that several major areas in psychology are concerned with problems of personality and behavior change (e.g., learning, social psychology, educational psychology) and that other disciplines (most notably, education) share similar concerns, we must ask ourselves what is unique about the professional activities of the psychotherapist.

There is a growing conviction (Goldstein, Heller, & Sechrest, 1966) that the therapist's psychological influence is basically identical with other forms of psychological influence so that research in psychotherapy should become firmly aligned with research in other areas concerned with similar problems. If this view is accepted, the mechanisms of psychological change which are at work in psychotherapy are intrinsically no different from those in the home, the classroom, and the political arena. The basic problem in psychotherapy therefore is *how one person influences another*, and this calls for the specification of the *conditions* which potentiate or, alternatively, vitiate the process. Simply put: What does the psychotherapist *do* to bring about a given *result?* As we have seen, in practice this question is anything but simple. We may also observe that theories of psychotherapy are attempts to explain in parsimonious terms the activities of the psychotherapist and the mechanisms by which he achieves personality and behavior change. As an empiricist, the researcher in psychotherapy is concerned more directly with what the therapist *does,* contrasted with what he *says* he does in terms of some theoretical beliefs.

We must also note that *the psychotherapist is a technician,* and psychotherapy in the final analysis is a *technology.* Schematically, the psychotherapist employs psychological principles to accomplish a certain aim, much as an engineer employs principles of physics to build a bridge. However, there is nothing in the principles of physics which says that they shall be used for constructive or destructive purposes. Similarly, psychological principles can be used constructively (e.g., by helping a person to become independent and free) and destructively (e.g., by dominating or oppressing him, as through brainwashing). These are not scientific but moral issues which will be discussed in greater detail elsewhere in this volume (Appendix A).

While the psychotherapist undoubtedly employs common ° psychological principles in his work, there are distinct differences between the psychotherapeutic situation and other interpersonal situations aimed at personality and behavior change. For one thing, unlike other psychological manipulators, the psychotherapist attempts to be keenly aware of the technical operations he employs in bringing about change in the patient and, at least in principle, he is highly goal directed. This is not to assert that the psychotherapist understands fully, or even adequately, the nature of the influence he is exerting, but he is continually concerned with the problem. Secondly, unlike any other human relationship, the psychotherapeutic situation is largely "uncontaminated" by the therapist's personal needs (such as approval, appreciation, etc.) as well as the niceties ordinarily expected in social intercourse. Apart from the payment of a professional fee and injunctions against destructive physical action, the patient is given unusual free-

° The term *common* is used in the sense of the preceding discussion. It does not mean that the principles or the conditions governing them are well understood.

dom of self-expression. For these reasons the therapeutic situation constitutes a unique laboratory situation in which the thoughts, feelings, and beliefs of the patient can be studied in a relatively "pure culture." As we have noted, it is a highly personal situation within a highly impersonal framework which conduces to honesty, frankness, and self-revelation not found anywhere else. Therefore, the possibility of studying and understanding basic psychological principles is infinitely greater in the two-person situation of psychotherapy than in any other setting. It is the author's conviction that the potentialities of this "interpersonal laboratory" have barely begun to be explored.

Returning to the study of psychotherapeutic techniques, the researcher must ask himself how the therapist's psychological influence is mediated and how it can be investigated. Superficially, the two participants exchange verbal communications, and the therapist's messages, over time, somehow have an effect on the patient's personality and actions. How does this happen? As soon as we examine the problem more closely we find that, as in other human interactions, the participants react not only to the verbal symbols but also to the attitudes they convey and other underlying meanings, such as suggestions for a course of action. The words do not occur in a vacuum but in the context of a relationship; that is, their meaning is partly determined by the feelings and attitudes of the participants toward each other as well as other aspects of the situation. The patient's attitude may be trusting or suspicious; the therapist may be perceived by the patient as warm, rejecting, neutral, impersonal, etc. For these reasons (and others) one is merely making a beginning (and perhaps a very feeble one) if he counts the frequency of words or characterizes the communications in terms of questions, interpretations, and so forth. In principle, the investigator would like to study the specific effects of a specific message, but this effort quickly bogs down if he focuses attention upon microscopic units, such as words or phrases. On the other hand, if he takes account of the broader context and attempts to summarize the transactions occurring, say, in a single hour, he cannot be sure which communications were potent and which were inert. Similarly, the patient's immediate reaction to a particular therapist communication cannot be accepted as an index of its effectiveness since reactions may be delayed and the effects of particular communications may be cumulative.

The foregoing are only some of the difficulties with which research aimed at the process of psychotherapy is beset. Nevertheless, researchers have invested considerable effort in the study of therapeutic transactions.

Research on techniques may be divided into two broad areas: (1) investigations which focus on the naturally occurring events in psychotherapy (so-called process studies); and (2) investigations in which technique variables are manipulated experimentally. The former area, historically the older, has been advanced through the development of systems of content analysis.

CONTENT ANALYSIS

As an indication of the growing significance of content analysis, the first major review of this area (Auld & Murray, 1955) covered about one hundred references, whereas more recent ones (Marsden, 1965; 1970) cite several times that number.

Content analysis was originally defined as "a research technique for the objective, systematic, and quantitative description of the manifest content of communication" (Berelson, 1952), but it has since been broadened to include the direct quantification of complex clinical concepts, linguistic and paralinguistic analysis, and the study of fine body movements (*kinesics*).

Research problems to which systems of content analysis have been addressed have included the description of patient behavior, therapist behavior, patient-therapist interaction, as well as inferences concerning internal, psychodynamic states, notably of patients.

Part of the work devoted to the analysis of patient communications has been supported by the general hypothesis that personality and behavior changes resulting from psychotherapy are paralleled by changes in the patient's verbalizations in therapy. In general, studies of this kind have yielded quantitative confirmation of the theoretical position from which they originated. For example, research within the client-centered framework has shown positive changes in the patient's self-concept over the course of therapy. Researchers have also succeeded in differentiating successful from less successful cases (Rogers, 1959; 1961) and in predicting outcome on the basis of the patient's manner of verbalization in early interviews (Rice, 1965).

Objective differences in theoretical orientation, experience level, and empathic ability are some therapist characteristics that have been studied in considerable detail. As might be expected, the therapist's experience level has generally been shown to have a positive relationship to outcome; however, the evidence is not unequivocal, and there persists the clinical observation that young, untutored but enthusiastic therapists are often more effective than seasoned practitioners. A sizable literature (Truax & Carkhuff, 1967) supports the view that empathic ability on the part of the therapist is associated with successful outcome. On the other hand, it has not been demonstrated that one theoretical approach is consistently superior to others.

Indirectly related to research involving content analysis are recent efforts to differentiate on the basis of quantitative measures "productive" from "nonproductive" therapy hours (Orlinsky & Howard, 1967; Auerbach, in progress; Strupp, Chassan, & Ewing, 1966).

A good deal of research dealing with the analysis of linguistic, paralinguistic, kinesic, and other modes of communication has been contributed in recent years. Pittenger, Hockett, and Danehy (1960), for example, carried out a linguistic analysis of the first five minutes of an initial interview which filled a fair-sized book. Despite advances in this area, progress has been slow because of the great amount of tedious effort required in dealing with microscopic interview segments and other problems (see above).

In numerous psychophysiological studies, measures of autonomic and skeletal-motor functions (e.g., heart rate, skin temperature, muscle potentials, and skin resistance) have been used as indicators of affect in therapeutic situations. Akin in some respects to lie-detection procedures, these measures have been intended as objective indicators of focal conflict areas, influence of the therapist's communications on the patient's affective state, qualitative changes in the patient-therapist relationship, and the like. While autonomic and skeletal-motor responses are sensitive indicators, they are also highly variable, and they have no simple meanings which can be read from a dial. On the contrary, they require difficult inferences concerning the psychological aspects of the therapeutic transaction.

EXPERIMENTAL MANIPULATIONS OF TECHNIQUE

Whereas the considerable body of research involving systems of content analysis has been heavily influenced by client-centered and psychoanalytic theory, the impetus for experimental manipulations of specified technique variables has come from researchers favoring behavioral approaches. The former kind of research has almost exclusively been performed in the therapeutic situation, whereas the latter has often been done in quasi-therapy settings.

The work by Matarazzo and his collaborators is an illustration of the manipulation of selected formal characteristics of the interview situation. In essence, these investigators programmed certain aspects of the verbal behavior of the interviewer. Matarazzo, Wiens, and Saslow (1965) assert that "noncontent measures, either alone or, more likely, in combination with content-derived psychotherapy measures, appear to have a higher than average probability of furthering our understanding of 'process' and related psychotherapy phenomena" [p. 209].

The burgeoning literature on verbal conditioning is supported by the following claims advanced by its proponents (Krasner, 1965): "Verbal conditioning is a major part of traditional psychotherapy and a 'treatment' procedure in its own right" [p. 226]. Originally, this work had as its aim the reinforcement of all emotional words through minimal social approval, such as head-nodding, smiling, "mm-hmm," and "good." Subsequently research became concerned with verbal conditioning as a direct form of psychotherapy. There is still considerable doubt about the extent to which verbal conditioning plays a *major* role in effecting personality and behavior change in psychotherapy.

In the context of social learning, the work of Bandura and his group (1965) demonstrates the value of modeling procedures and vicarious learning in modifying behavior. The therapist, as part of his technical repertoire, undoubtedly models attitudes and behaviors which are learned by the patient, and it will be useful to explore in greater detail the extent to which these techniques are important in therapeutic learning.

Summary

As we have seen, a great deal of research has been concerned with the description and measurement of therapeutic techniques. This work has proceeded on the reasonable assumption that psychotherapy must be understood in terms of the ongoing interaction between the two participants. Two general approaches have been differentiated: (1) studies concerned with analyses of the interview content, and (2) the construction of laboratory or quasi-therapy situations in which one mechanism is manipulated systematically.

Contemporary research on techniques rejects broad categorizations (such as *psychoanalytic* or *client-centered*) as insufficiently descriptive of the actual transactions. In this connection, Ford and Urban state:

> When one examines the descriptions of how free association, inquiry, or relationship are implemented, one finds these conceptual labels refer to fairly elaborate sets of procedures. Each is not an operation, but a whole set of interrelated events. . . . Thus, speaking about technique in such general terms tends to obscure the heterogeneity of procedures actually used and reduces the precision with which therapeutic operations can be communicated to others [1963, pp. 675–677].

To a large extent the future of psychotherapy hinges upon the refinement of existing techniques and the development of new ones. The repertoire of the contemporary psychotherapist includes a variety of techniques which often are employed more or less intuitively and unsystematically. No form of psychotherapy can lay claim to using one technique exclusively, although schools of therapy differ in their relative emphases upon particular techniques. Future research must seek to refine the measurement of techniques and to assess their effects under specified conditions. Major difficulties impeding the realization of this goal have been delineated.

Suggested Readings

BERGIN, A. E.   The effects of psychotherapy: Negative results revisited. *Journal of Counseling Psychology,* 1963, **10**, 244–250.

BERGIN, A. E.   Some implications of psychotherapy research for therapeutic practice. *Journal of Abnormal Psychology,* 1966, **71**, 235–246.

BERGIN, A. E., & GARFIELD, S. (Eds.)   *Handbook of psychotherapy and behavior change: An empirical analysis.* New York: Wiley, 1970.

BORDIN, E. S.   The personality of the therapist as an influence in psychotherapy. In M. J. Feldman (Ed.), *Studies in psychotherapy and behavioral change*. Buffalo: State University of New York, 1968. Pp. 37–54.

CAMPBELL, D. T., & STANLEY, J.   *Experimental and quasi-experimental designs for research*. Chicago: Rand McNally, 1963.

KRASNER, L.   The therapist as a social reinforcement machine. In H. H. Strupp & L. Luborsky (Eds.), *Research in psychotherapy*. Vol. 2. Washington, D. C.: American Psychological Association, 1962. Pp. 61–94.

LUBORSKY, L.   The patient's personality and psychotherapeutic change. In H. H. Strupp & L. Luborsky (Eds.), *Research in psychotherapy*. Vol. 2. Washington, D. C.: American Psychological Association, 1962. Pp. 115–133.

MARSDEN, G.   Content analysis studies of psychotherapy. In A. E. Bergin & S. L. Garfield (Eds.), *Handbook of psychotherapy and behavior change: An empirical analysis*. New York: Wiley, 1970.

MATARAZZO, J. D., WIENS, A. N., & SASLOW, G.   Studies in interview speech behavior. In L. Krasner & L. P. Ullmann (Eds.), *Research in behavior modification: New developments and their clinical implications*. New York: Holt, 1965. Pp. 179–210.

ROGERS, C. R., GENDLIN, E. T., KIESLER, D., & TRUAX, C. B.   *The therapeutic relationship and its impact: A study of psychotherapy with schizophrenics*. Madison: University of Wisconsin Press, 1967.

SARGENT, H. D.   Intrapsychic change: Methodological problems in psychotherapy research. *Psychiatry*, 1961, 24, 93–108.

STRUPP, H. H.   *Psychotherapists in action: Explorations of the therapist's contribution to the treatment process*. New York: Grune & Stratton, 1960.

STRUPP, H. H.   Patient-doctor relationships: Psychotherapists in the therapeutic process. In A. H. Bachrach (Ed.), *Experimental foundations of clinical psychology*. New York: Basic Books, 1962. Pp. 576–615.

STRUPP, H. H., & BERGIN, A. E.   Some empirical and conceptual bases for coordinated research in psychotherapy. *International Journal of Psychiatry*, 1969, 7, 18–90.

CHAPTER 8

PSYCHOTHERAPY: PROBLEMS
AND PERSPECTIVES

Place of Psychotherapy in Psychology

S cientific psychology in America is frequently criticized for being insufficiently responsive to the serious human problems confronting our society which are seen by many people as threatening our very survival. Some critics (e.g., Bakan, 1969) point to the massive literature dealing with problems of learning (estimated at 50,000 to 100,000 journal articles), one of the major topics of academic psychology, and assert that there is very little in this work which can be applied to education and to the problems people face in getting along with each other. Large numbers of college students turn to courses in psychology for the purpose of obtaining a better understanding of themselves, their contemporaries, their elders, and society. Yet they often find the subject matter barren and the textbooks uninspiring. Even abnormal psychology, long one of the favorite fields within psychology, provides little that is helpful to the student for his personal development and in his efforts to find his place in a complex and conflict-ridden world. Psychotherapy, however, is a notable exception. There are few concerns in psychology which have proved as thought-provoking, challenging, and productive of valuable insights as psychotherapy, with its emphasis on the inner man, his strivings for self-realization and self-actualization, and the perennial problems of his existence. Whereas other branches of psychology have focused on part-processes, like memory, learning, and perception, psychotherapy has been concerned with man as a living being and it has been sensitive to his struggles with himself and others.

Paradoxically, while uniquely focused on significant psychological problems, psychotherapy has never been embraced by academic psychology, nor has it encountered cordial acceptance by medicine. Freud, for example, had virtually no ties to academic psychology as it was taught and studied at German universities in the nineteenth century, and medicine rejected psychoanalysis with even stronger vehemence. In part this was undoubtedly a function of Freud's discoveries, which confronted man with unpleasant truths about himself, his attacks on hypocrisy and "the establishment," as well as his insistence on the need for uncompromising honesty in exploring man's motives and aspirations. As a result of this animosity, he was forced to create separate institutes for training therapists; he had to start new journals to publish his findings; and he had to reconcile himself to a fringe existence in the academic community. Nevertheless, he never ceased to insist that psychoanalysis is a part of psychology, not of abnormal psychology, but of general psychology.

With the rise of clinical psychology as a profession following World War II psychoanalytic concepts began to permeate American psychology, but despite a certain enthusiasm for psychodiagnostic testing which borrowed heavily from psychoanalytic teachings (notably in the well-known Rorschach test and other projective techniques), this trend proved relatively short-lived. It came increasingly under criticism from investigators who were disillusioned by the fact that, useful as these techniques are in the hands of some insightful clinicians, their predictive power is severely limited, and in group comparisons their validity is at best modest.

The emergence of nondirective or client-centered therapy, together with its emphasis on the empirical study of therapeutic phenomena, greatly enhanced the status of psychotherapy within American psychology, and the teachings of Rogers and those of other phenomenologists (including existential or humanistic therapists) began to overshadow psychoanalysis, which, except in the large urban centers where it continues to enjoy acceptance, again fell into disrepute.

EXPERIENTIAL LEARNING VERSUS BEHAVIOR MODIFICATION

In the 1960s a new trend began to emerge in the form of behavior psychotherapy, which to many American psychologists appears to meet the need for (1) efficiency in producing therapeutic results; (2) emphasis on empirical and experimental study; (3) theoretical parsimony; and (4) articulating the principles of therapeutic learning to traditional concerns of academic psychology. With respect to the last point, psychotherapy has come to be seen not as an esoteric enterprise with conceptualizations and processes peculiarly its own, but as an area in which the principles of general psychology (social learning, cognitive learning, etc.) can be fruitfully applied.

The most basic question confronting the psychotherapist as well as the researcher may be phrased as follows: Is psychotherapy primarily a *significant experience in living* or is it a *technology* by which changes in personality and behavior can be brought about? The issue, as we shall see, has far-reaching implications not only for the practice of psychotherapy, but also for the directions and form of investigative efforts, examples of which have been examined in this volume. Lastly, the question has a bearing on the kind of science psychology is today and purports to be tomorrow.

Let us examine the second alternative first: Behaviorally oriented therapists and researchers, as reflected in the new term "behavior modification," view themselves as technicians. For them the future of psychotherapy lies in the development of a technology which permits planned changes in a person's maladaptive behavior. If this view is accepted, what the field needs to do is to concentrate attention on specific symptoms or problems in living, to define the conditions which sustain and perpetuate these behaviors, and to develop efficient and focused methods for effecting their modification. Implicitly, if not explicitly, behavior therapists are not concerned with the person of the client, his life goals, his view of the world, beliefs, convictions, and desires. They do not deny the existence of man's inner world, but they regard it as outside the province of the behavioral scientist.

Interestingly, psychoanalysis, while diametrically opposed to behaviorism in significant respects, shares its emphasis on "mechanisms" and their control. Essentially, the psychoanalytically oriented therapist is concerned with impersonal forces over which the patient has no control but which are seen as powerfully influencing his feelings and behavior. Perhaps for highly personal and temperamental reasons, Freud eschewed imposing his beliefs and values upon the patient, and while he acknowledged that the therapist at times has to serve the patient as a model and mentor, he likened the therapist's job to that of a surgeon who seeks to correct malfunctions of the body through precise and technical interventions. The patient *as a human being* is not the surgeon's concern. According to Freud, it is not the psychotherapist's, either. What the therapist needs to do is to understand the forces which sustain intrapsychic conflicts and to bring about a more viable balance.

THERAPEUTIC PRACTICE VERSUS RESEARCH

If this view is accepted, the future of psychotherapy is that of a scientific technology. Just as it has been possible to study in impersonal terms the forces at work in lightning and thunder, it should be possible to study the mechanisms of psychological influence in much the same way. The goal then is to understand these forces, to describe the conditions under which they clash or function harmoniously, and to develop techniques for their orderly alignment. Consequently, we are developing a psychology which is not concerned with personal idiosyncrasies or the uniqueness of the individual but with lawful psychological processes reduced to their lowest possible common denominator. In this approach psychology becomes patterned after the older and more respected natural sciences, and there may be the hope that some day its technological achievements will be equally impressive. Perhaps it does not necessarily follow that such a science must focus its attention *exclusively* on *observable* behavior (as opposed to private, subjective experience), a conclusion the behaviorists have drawn, but in the course of such a program the uniqueness of man is almost certainly destined to be eroded. Research in psychotherapy, as it is emerging in this country, typically follows this tradition, exemplified by an emphasis on empirical data, experimental manipulations, and observable changes in behavior.

TWO VIEWS

1. The personal experience. The exponent of the view that psychotherapy must deal with the irreducible uniqueness of the individual might express his position in the following terms:

> Psychotherapy, first and foremost, is a *clinical art, not a science*. My task is to aid and promote personality growth or, more accurately, to help a troubled human being in his struggle with his emotional difficulties. I assume that the patient is fully capable of steering his own life course once the obstacles which stand in his way are removed. My task is to aid him in this process. I don't "handle" a case, I don't "manipulate" a person, I don't apply a "technique." My whole effort is concentrated upon *understanding* this person and his difficulties in living. From this vantage point, I don't see how it would help me to know that persons having certain psychological characteristics are better candidates for intensive psychotherapy than persons having some other characteristics; that interpretations of a certain kind tend to produce resistance in certain kinds of patients at a certain stage in therapy; that under certain conditions the therapist's personal problems tend to interfere with the therapeutic process; that certain patterns of personality characteristics in a therapist are more conducive to progress in therapy than certain oth-

ers; that interpretive techniques are more effective in the hands of certain therapists with certain kinds of patients under certain circumstances. How do such findings help me to understand my patient whom I am seeing three times a week, who relates to me, a particular therapist, in a particular way, who tells me about his anxieties in highly specific situations and whose style of life, defensive patterns, life goals, fantasies, and wishes are a unique constellation? True, there are important clinical papers which have influenced me deeply: They are the papers of a host of sensitive therapists—not the kinds of investigations which are based on a sample of patients often treated by student therapists, which report results at the .05 or .01 level of statistical confidence. I am in sympathy with the point of view which says that we must achieve greater clarity about our concepts and our operations, but I doubt whether an experimenter standing *outside* the therapeutic situation can deepen my understanding of patients as living human beings.

In the same vein, Rogers views the therapeutic relationship "as a heightening of the constructive qualities which often exist in part in other relationships, and an extension through time of qualities which in other relationships tend at best to be momentary" [1957, p. 101]. He concludes that "the techniques of the various therapies are relatively unimportant" [1957, p. 102] and, stressing the overriding importance of the therapist's attitudes, asserts:

> Any of the techniques may communicate the fact that the therapist is expressing one attitude at a surface level, and another contradictory attitude which is denied to his own awareness. Thus one value of such a theoretical formulation as we have offered is that it may assist therapists to think more critically about those elements of their experience, attitudes, and behaviors which are essential to psychotherapy, and those which are nonessential or even deleterious to psychotherapy [1957, p. 103].

The present author, addressing himself to the same problem, has stated:

> [The therapist's] personal attributes (maturity, warmth, acceptance, etc.) enable him to create the kind of interpersonal relationship in which constructive personality change can take place; his knowledge of psychodynamic principles permits him, in and through his relationship, to initiate the kinds of emotional unlearning and learning experiences that are considered necessary to the alleviation or resolution of neurotic conflicts. The latter would be impossible without the former; the former, by itself, would never be sufficient [Strupp, 1958, p. 66].

2. The humanistic position. ° Within humanistic psychology, a recent development in psychotherapy with deep roots in existentialist philosophy, the psychotherapeutic situation is seen as an encounter between two *persons*. The patient is regarded as an individual with problems in living but also as a human being striving to realize his potentialities. The therapist is viewed not as an analytic manipulator or technician but as a human being who, aided by technical training and experience in living, attempts to *understand* the patient as a person. This understanding is to be accomplished through emotional participation in living with the other person over an extended period of time, to the end that the therapist's influence conduces to constructive personality growth. The focus is upon the *experiential* components of the situation, to which everything else becomes subordinate, including the technical operations by which the experience is facilitated.

In explicating the humanistic point of view to American readers, one author states:

> Existential analysis is a way of understanding human existence, and its representatives believe that one of the chief (if not *the* chief) blocks to the understanding of human beings in Western culture is precisely the overemphasis on technique, an overemphasis which goes along with the tendency to see the human being as an object to be calculated, managed, analyzed. [May, Angel, & Ellenberger, 1958, p. 76].

The central issue is "whether the human being is an object to be analyzed or a being to be understood" [May, Angel, & Ellenberger, 1958, p. 81].

In May's words, this conception of the therapeutic relationship

> . . . is in no way an over-simplification or short cut; it is not a substitute for discipline or thoroughness of training. It rather puts these things in their context—namely, discipline and thoroughness of training directed to understanding human beings as human. The therapist is assumedly an expert; but, if he is not first of all a human being, his expertness will be irrelevant and quite possibly harmful. The distinctive character of the existential approach is that understanding *being human* is no longer just a "gift," an intuition, or something left to chance; it is the "proper study

---

° This position seems to be more a philosophical approach than it is a system of psychotherapy. For this reason it has not been discussed in a separate chapter in this book.

of man [Mankind]," in Alexander Pope's phrase, and becomes the center of a thorough and scientific concern in the broad sense. The existential analysts do the same thing with the structure of human existence that Freud did with the structure of the unconscious—namely, take it out of the realm of the hit-and-miss gift of special intuitive individuals, accept it as the area of exploration and understanding, and make it to some extent teachable [1958, pp. 82–83].

If one follows this view it would be of little avail to investigate whether psychotherapy works or even whether one technique is more effective than another. Rather one would have to ask: *Is this particular therapist, by virtue of being a particular person, capable of creating the kinds of conditions in which a given technique or techniques can attain their maximum usefulness?* The question of the relative effectiveness of technique still has to be answered; but the primary focus, according to the existentialist position, is on the *person* of the therapist by whom a particular technique is used. Can he understand the patient as a human being struggling with life's problems? Can he communicate this understanding to the end that the patient feels deeply understood? For methodological reasons, research may emphasize one aspect or the other, but the totality of therapist and technique in interaction with a particular patient cannot be ignored.

It would appear necessary to find ways and means to conduct investigations which do justice both to the demands of scientific rigor and the depth and breadth of the therapeutic undertaking. To this end, researchers must become better and more insightful clinicians, and clinicians must develop a greater awareness of the ideals which the scientist espouses. Among other things, such a rapprochement may result in a larger number of research contributions that are meaningful and relevant to the therapist. Similarly, it may inspire that tentativeness, caution, and respect for error in human observation which is still seen lacking in many clinicians.

The subject-object split that still pervades the science of psychology seems a particularly grave obstacle to the interpenetration of clinical practice and research in psychology. Russell (1948), quoted by Szasz (1957), has eloquently dealt with this issue and defined psychology as a science dealing with essentially private experience. Among psychologists, Allport (1955) has criticized the prevailing behaviorist tendency to regard the human person as "empty." In the area of psychotherapy, the investigations of Rogers and his students are perhaps the best illustration that fruitful research on the process of psychotherapy can be done, while retaining something of the uniqueness of the persons participating in the process (Rogers & Dymond, 1954). These are but beginnings, but they seem important beginnings in studying objectively the subjective experiences of patient and therapist in interaction.

Erwin Straus' dictum that "Whatever is related to my particular existence lessens and obscures knowledge" [May, Angel, & Ellenberger, 1958, p. 145] seems to center on a dilemma in research on psychotherapy. In order to expand scientific knowledge of the therapeutic process, *it is necessary to objectify essentially subjective experiences;* but as one succeeds in doing so, one runs the danger of sacrificing the essence of what one is studying. Therefore, the obverse of the quotation likewise appears to be true: Knowledge lessens and obscures whatever is related to my particular existence. This, of course, is precisely what science attempts to do in all areas of investigation. Is psychotherapy an exception? If so, it can hardly become a science. If not, the search for invariance amidst change must go forward— common elements must be abstracted, and the unique aspects of the therapeutic encounter may have to be ignored. In one sense, the future *may* bring the development of techniques for *simultaneously* achieving both objectives. This is a hope which may never materialize, and it may in principle be an impossibility. In that event, the therapist and the researcher in psychotherapy may move further apart, unless the clinician abandons his commitments, which seems as unlikely as the researcher forsaking the ideals of science.

How Can the Researcher Proceed?

The preceding considerations have important implications for the advancement of knowledge in psychotherapy and the kinds of research strategies to be employed toward this end. In keeping with the distinction between "clinicians" and "researchers," a similar distinction in terms of their approach to research may be made between *naturalistic observation* and *experimentation*.

As we have seen in the early chapters of this volume, psychotherapy as it is practiced, understood, and conceptualized today is largely the creation of insightful clinicians who made significant discoveries about emotional problems in the context of the two-person interaction. Like Darwin, Freud observed natural phenomena, abstracted general principles from his observations on relatively few subjects, and constructed a complex theory, in his case of personality development and psychotherapy, from these data. His work did not grow out of experimentation in the laboratory but was in the tradition of healing. However, he looked at the phenomena objectively, realizing more clearly than anyone before his time that objectivity in the interpersonal realm is extraordinarily difficult to achieve and that this fact in itself constitutes one of the major obstacles to research in the area. Furthermore, his thinking was guided by experience. Science always must be built on empirical data, not necessarily on experimentation, a distinction which is frequently misunderstood. Many sciences were for a long time empirical before they became experimental, and experimentation, together with precise measurement, is often one of the late developments in the history of a science.

Naturalistic observation in the hands of perceptive and creative men can lead to revolutionary discoveries, but it can also lead into blind alleys. The truth is that in the final analysis scientific discoveries are the product of creative minds who can isolate important principles while disregarding idiosyncratic aspects of complex phenomena. Others, less creative, may look at the same phenomena without ever being able to separate the wheat from the chaff. In short, there is no guaranteed *method* for generating insights, and the creative process remains shrouded in mystery.

Research always starts with a question. Observations then lead to inferences or generalizations, from which predictions may be made. Predictions are confirmed or disconfirmed by further observation (Woodger, 1956).

Typical questions in psychotherapy are: What is the nature of the patient's problem? What can be done to eliminate or ameliorate it? These were starting points for Freud and Breuer's work, and it followed the course sketched above. Other clinicians have viewed the problem along different lines, and they evolved different techniques for modifying it.

Among the difficulties with naturalistic observation are its inherent imprecision (although methods have been developed for refining and systematizing observations) and the perennial question pertaining to the generalizability of observations made on an individual case. That is, the clinician may believe that he has isolated an important principle if he finds evidence supporting his hypothesis in patients 1, 2, and 3; but the next patient may provide him with contradictory evidence. Freud was fortunate because on the basis of rather limited observations he was able to abstract principles which, at least in a broad sense, turned out to be correct. However, the complexity of human beings typically defies the isolation of specific principles and the repetition (replication) of observations.

The great advantage of the naturalistic approach is its minimal interference with the phenomena under study, which in turn permits their scrutiny in a broad context. Terms like *molar, holistic, field-observational* are frequently used to characterize this method.

EXPERIMENTAL APPROACH

The experimental approach, as we have seen, is characterized by the isolation and manipulation of single (or very few) variables under closely controlled conditions, and it is frequently termed *molecular, atomistic,* or *reductionistic.* Much research in American psychology (less so on the European continent) follows this model, which is regarded by many researchers as the royal road to scientific discovery and knowledge. The experimental approach places great weight on the proper design of a study, techniques for controlling variables, precise measurement, and the application of statistical methods for assessing the outcomes of a study. The last half century has witnessed the evolution of sophisticated experimental designs and methods of statistical analysis which are employed by psychologists and other behavioral scientists in their work. A number of studies that have been described in earlier chapters illustrate the methods as well as the goals of the experimental approach, which has been applied to research in psychotherapy only during the last two or three decades.

The Researcher's Dilemma: Complexity versus Control

The naturalistic-experimental distinction is of course schematic, and in practice the two approaches are not mutually exclusive. For example, it is possible to introduce experimental manipulations in the context of a naturalistic clinical interaction; and it is likewise possible to make naturalistic observations in a closely controlled experimental setting.

Nevertheless in psychotherapy research the two approaches have often been pitted against each other, and their relative merits have been argued. Essentially, we are confronted with a dilemma which takes the following form: On the one hand, one may observe therapeutic phenomena in a clinical setting; that is, in a situation designed for the purpose of helping a disturbed individual. In that event, the helping attitude of the therapist must remain uppermost and the totality of his procedures and interventions must be geared to helping the patient overcome his problem in living in the most expeditious and efficacious way. Consequently, the clinician's investigative interests become subordinated to the therapeutic objective. If he proceeds in this manner, he has the opportunity to study the broad spectrum of the patient's feelings, attitudes, and emotional reactions in a naturalistic (clinical) context, but he cannot manipulate experimentally a single variable to study its effect except insofar as a particular research procedure may be made a part of his therapeutic objectives. This is the single-case approach as it has been practiced by psychotherapists since the advent of modern psychotherapy. It can be readily seen that the clinician is always confronted with a welter of variables which he cannot hope to control, and he is continually faced with their complicated interactions. True, he can exert a limited amount of control over the situation through his own objectivity, and he may avoid getting emotionally involved with the patient, but he is always dealing with the total human being. In this way he is observing "nature"; that is, a *real* patient in trouble who is seeking help from an expert.

The experimental approach, by contrast, requires a setting in which one or a very small number of variables can be manipulated and the effects of the experimental procedure studied. As we have seen, rigorous control is extremely difficult to achieve in the clinical situation.

For this reason many investigators have turned to so-called analogues; that is, situations in which the real-life events of psychotherapy are simulated. The present author (Strupp, 1958; 1965), for example, in order to study therapists' attitudinal and emotional reactions to a patient presented clinicians with a sound film of a therapeutic interview, and the respondents were asked to assume that they were interviewing and interacting with a real patient. In this way it was possible to study the reactions of a large sample of viewers all of whom responded to the identical stimulus situation. Thus differences in response style were a function of the viewers' personality characteristics, which were under investigation in these studies.

The drawbacks of this form of research revolve largely around the artificiality of the experimental situation and the resulting uncertainty of whether observations made in this setting are applicable to real-life therapeutic situations. That is, the validity of experimental analogues is indeterminate. At one extreme, there may be a close correspondence between a therapist's behavior in the experimental situation and in real life; at the other, the experimental situation may have produced such distortions as to invalidate the results. In most studies the truth probably lies somewhere between these extremes, but ordinarily one does not know where. There are techniques for studying the question of validity (for example, through a series of investigations, a variety of settings, comparisons between a therapist's behavior in the laboratory and in actual therapy), but there always remains an element of doubt concerning the generalizability of findings obtained in an experimental situation. To return once again to the studies mentioned above, one may ask: Does a therapist confronted with a real patient in his office react identically (or similarly) as he did to the patient he viewed in the film: What can be said about a therapist's "relationship" to a filmed patient who does not respond to the therapist-viewer and on whom the therapist's hypothetical communications have no impact? To what extent are the therapist's responses in the experimental situation distorted by the so-called demand characteristics of the situation—that is, his views about the purpose of the experiment, expectations about the experimenter's intentions, etc.? Even if the therapist-viewer reacted similarly to a real patient having the characteristics of the film patient, to what patient characteristics is he responding? Would he react to all of his real patients in the same way? In short, an experimental analogue may raise more questions than it answers, and precision and experimental control may have been purchased at the cost of realism.

The dilemma, therefore, may be formulated as follows: *The greater the realism of the situation, the less it is possible to isolate variables and subject them to experimental manipulation. Contrariwise, the greater the experimental control over single variables, the greater the artificiality of the situation and the more questionable the validity of the results obtained under those conditions.* The problem may be likened to efforts of studying the physiological activity of a cell under a microscope, assuming the cell cannot be placed under a microscope while the organism is alive. If the experimenter kills the organism he may be able to examine the cell, but he has lost the opportunity to study a biological process. Similarly, in psychotherapy research there is a serious question whether the complex interaction between a trained therapist and a troubled patient can be simulated in any other setting. By the same token, comparisons between any given patient-therapist pair are rendered difficult because no two pairs are ever alike and they may not even be comparable. Therefore group comparisons encounter obstacles similar to the ones pertaining to the naturalistic-experimental dilemma.

RENEWED INTEREST IN THE STUDY OF THE SINGLE CASE

A partial solution to the problem may be found through the intensive study of single cases in the natural clinical setting, but instead of relying solely on the clinician's (frequently fallible) impressions, engaging in efforts to refine, systematize, and perhaps even quantify observations (Chassan, 1967). Furthermore, audio and video recording techniques (while introducing a certain amount of distortion) can be used to present the patient-therapist interactions to external observers for close study. Finally, after having obtained better descriptions of the variables it may be possible to introduce experimental manipulations into the clinical situation and to observe their effects.

This approach takes account of the complexity of the clinical situation but tries to introduce greater rigor into the clinical observations. At the same time it seeks to combine the naturalistic with the experimental approach. The solution was termed "partial" because it does not resolve in a decisive way the problems which have been enumerated, although it may be a very reasonable compromise for the clinical investigator. Increasingly, researchers in psychotherapy have realized that research in the behavioral sciences, while sharing common objectives with scientific research in the physical and natural sciences, faces uncommonly difficult and perhaps unique problems with which we are as yet inadequately equipped to deal. Advances in technology (e.g., computers and recording instruments) will undoubtedly aid but they cannot supplant ingenuity, creativity, and insights. The answer ultimately lies in nurturing and fostering an inquiring attitude among young scientists and in acquainting them with the exorbitantly difficult but also challenging problems in psychology.

Conclusion

The questions raised at the beginning of this chapter still loom large. It is disquieting to contemplate the large discrepancy between clinical and philosophical insights, on the one hand, and research accomplishments, on the other. As researchers, we seem to lack methods for making greater inroads on the phenomena with which psychotherapy deals—the broad spectrum of human experience. For instance: How do we assess and measure such qualities in the therapist as: respect for the patient's struggle toward self-realization and self-direction; capacity for empathy; warmth; acceptance of the humanness of another person; depth of *Weltanschauung* (world view) and life experience; emotional maturity; ability to serve as a model of reality—all of which undoubtedly play an important role in determining the extent to which the therapist can participate in and collaborate with the patient's striving for realizing his human potentialities. By contrast, the quantitative and comparative analyses of technique, formidable as they are, appear like child's play.

The fact that techniques for measuring significant personality attributes are in their infancy does not mean that they are doomed to remain there. The fact that so far the contributions from researchers to psychotherapeutic theory and practice have been modest may merely reflect an early stage of scientific development. The task poses a challenge to the imagination of researchers. We must show greater penetration in our research and refuse to purchase precision in measurement at the expense of shallowness of concepts. If we accept the proposition that psychotherapy's future is that of a scientific discipline, we have no choice but to undertake the laborious and painful drudgery of checking the empirical value of the clinical insights glimpsed by the pioneers and to sharpen our research instruments that they may become adequate to deal with the phenomena in this domain. At the turn of the century, modern psychotherapy emerged as a science largely because of the insights of Freud and other pioneers. Systematic work to test the original hypotheses was not begun until around 1940. Difficult as controlled research on these problems will be, the limits surely have not been tested. In the end, a balance must be achieved between scientific rigor and the richness and subtle complexity of human experience.

Suggested Readings

ALLPORT, G. W. *Becoming.* New Haven, Conn.: Yale, 1955.

BAKAN, D. *On method.* San Francisco: Jossey-Bass, 1967.

BREGER, L. The ideology of behaviorism. In L. Breger (Ed.), *Clinical-cognitive psychology.* Englewood Cliffs, N. J.: Prentice-Hall, 1969. Pp. 25–55.

BRIDGMAN, P. W. *The way things are.* Cambridge, Mass.: Harvard, 1959.

BUGENTAL, J. F. T. (Ed.) *Challenges of humanistic psychology.* New York: McGraw-Hill, 1967.

FORD, D. H., & URBAN, H. B. *Systems of psychology.* New York: Wiley, 1963.

FRANK, J. D. *Persuasion and healing.* Baltimore: Johns Hopkins, 1961.

KUHN, T. H. *The structure of scientific revolutions.* Chicago: University of Chicago, 1962.

MAY, R., ANGEL, E., & ELLENBERGER, H. F. (Eds.) *Existence.* New York: Basic Books, 1958.

OPPENHEIMER, J. R. *Science and the common understanding.* New York: Simon and Schuster, 1954.

POLANYI, M. *The tacit dimension.* New York: Doubleday, 1966.

ROGERS, C. R.   *On becoming a person.* Boston: Houghton Mifflin, 1961.

ROGERS, C. R., & Skinner, B. F.   Some issues concerning the control of human behavior: A symposium. *Science,* 1956, **124,** 1057–1066.

SZASZ, T. S.   *The ethics of psychoanalysis.* New York: Basic Books, 1965.

WANN, T. W. (Ed.)   *Behaviorism and phenomenology: Contrasting bases for modern psychology.* Chicago: University of Chicago, 1964.

APPENDIX A

Some Questions of Ethics

Whatever the effective ingredients of psychotherapy may turn out to be, it is clear that the *intent* of any psychotherapeutic intervention is to influence the feelings, attitudes, or the behavior of another person by psychological techniques. As soon as we recognize this fact, we begin to see considerable similarities between psychotherapy and propaganda, brainwashing, religious conversion, faith healing, and some aspects of the educational process aimed at indoctrinating the student with certain values. These parallels have been explored in detail by Frank (1961) and others. Psychological techniques for influencing another person are of course neither good nor evil in themselves, but the purposes for which they are employed have definite moral implications. It is to be noted that all techniques are ostensibly used for the purpose of "helping" the recipient although the notion of "help" is open to a variety of interpretations. In a free society adults have the right to accept help or to reject it, even when the latter alternative may be detrimental to themselves (as measured by some standards). For example, a patient may consult a physician for some medical problem, and the doctor may outline a course of treatment. He is also obligated to acquaint the patient with the nature of the treatment and the risks involved, as well as the dangers that may be expected from letting the condition go untreated. Nevertheless, the patient has the final choice, and when he agrees he gives informed consent. Except in emergencies where a family member may be required to consent to an operation because the patient is unconscious or otherwise completely incapacitated, the patient is the master of his own fate. How does this apply to psychotherapy?

The situation is relatively simple when the patient is an independent adult who consults a psychotherapist for the purpose of remedying some aspect of his personality which he has found troublesome. As we have seen, he may seek help for such symptoms as anxiety attacks, depressions, compulsive actions, undue timidity or shyness, recurrent conflicts with persons in authority, and many others. If the therapist agrees to accept the person for psychotherapy and the patient agrees, they enter into a contract (Szasz, 1965). As is true of any contractual agreement, the conditions should be explicit and spelled out clearly in advance. The therapist, for his part, agrees to meet with the patient for specified periods of time, during which he obligates himself to devote his best efforts to the patient's problems and to respect his confidences. In consideration of the time and the therapist's skill a fee is established. The payment of the fee is the patient's only obligation toward the therapist. This structure of the situation has far-reaching implications.

First, the patient remains an autonomous person throughout psychotherapy. He can use the therapist's verbal and nonverbal communications in any way he sees fit. In the course of the therapeutic work he may wish to change jobs, get married or divorced, or do nothing. He is also at liberty to terminate the therapeutic relationship at any time. The point is that the therapist does not assume responsibility for the patient's conduct nor does he advise him how to lead his life. His task is restricted to the clarification of meanings in the patient's communications, particularly recurrent tendencies, common in all patients, to turn the therapeutic relationship into a parent-child relationship or something else which it is not. Indeed, the correction of such distortions is central to the therapist's task.

Second, the absence of any obligation beyond the payment of a fee gives both parties an unusual degree of freedom. The patient owes the therapist nothing beyond money for his time and skill, and the therapist is not obligated to the patient. The relationship is one between two freely consenting adults, and it is a contractual or business relationship. The therapist has no obligation to "cure" the patient nor is the patient obligated to be "cured." By the same token, there is no need for the therapist to "love" the patient; the patient, however, has a right to feel respected and to be treated as an equal.

The emphasis on the contractual character of the therapeutic relationship further requires that the two parties be maximally frank and honest with each other in their dealings. One aspect of this requirement is an explicit understanding of the patient's and the therapist's roles, particularly what the patient may expect from therapy and the therapist. It has been shown (Riessman, Cohen, & Pearl, 1964) that most patients, especially members of the lower social classes, have exceedingly hazy notions of the process of psychotherapy, the role they are to play, and the kinds of outcomes that may be expected. The only model they typically can fall back on is the physician-patient relationship in which the patient is the passive recipient of the doctor's ministrations. This model is inapplicable to psychotherapy and can be grossly misleading. Researchers at the Phipps Psychiatric Clinic (Hoehn-Saric et al., 1964) have experimented with a role-induction interview preceding the patient's first meeting with the therapist. The purpose of the interview was to prepare the prospective patient for psychotherapy by acquainting him with the psychotherapeutic process and to dispel ignorance and misapprehensions. They found that such an interview had beneficial effects on the subsequent course of therapy and its outcome. To some extent, of course, such an interview interferes with the spontaneous emergence of distortions which themselves may provide extremely important grist for the therapeutic mill, but in short-term psychotherapy with lower class patients (as was true at Phipps), the role-induction procedure seemed to expedite the therapeutic work. In any event, the patient has a right to know something about the "mystery" of psychotherapy in advance, just as he has a right to know something about a surgical procedure that is recommended to him. He is also entitled to be enlightened about the therapist's qualifications. In practice the patient frequently is not told. The large dropout rate observed in clinics—not uncommonly more than 60 percent of the patients do not return for a second interview—may in part be traceable to misunderstandings on both sides. If the expectable gains from psychotherapy are uncertain (as they are) and if the patient is dealing with a therapist of limited experience (which is typically the case in a clinic), it seems no more than fair to inform him of these facts. Thus, both parties may be spared disappointments. But the patient cannot decide unless he is informed. This requirement derives from a sense of fair play and is basic to honesty in good interpersonal relations, of which the psychotherapeutic relationship purports to be a model. How can the patient learn to become more honest with himself if the professional helper does not abide by the same principles? Furthermore, how can he be taught to become a more independent, autonomous, and responsible adult, if he is not treated as one from the beginning of therapy? This conception of the therapeutic relationship is one of Freud's signal contributions and one which will undoubtedly be of lasting value.

Consider, by contrast, the situation of the involuntary patient. This group comprises prominently individuals confined in state mental hospitals, but includes also children and patients referred through a court of law. The case of children is not really relevant to this discussion because they are the wards of their parents who have the right to send them to a psychotherapist just as they have the right to choose a school, decide the need for medical treatment, etc. The situation is different, however, for the mental hospital patient and persons convicted of a crime, often a sexual offense. Not infrequently such persons have been given a suspended sentence with the proviso that they undergo psychiatric treatment, which may include psychotherapy.

Does an adult, whether he is a mental hospital patient, a convicted criminal, or subject to the jurisdiction of other authority, have the right to refuse psychotherapy? What is the position of the psychotherapist vis-à-vis such nonconsenting persons? Despite some notable exceptions (Szasz, 1963; 1965) the complex legal, ethical, and psychological issues have received inadequate attention by psychotherapists. In the present context it is sufficient to point out that serious questions must be raised about psychotherapeutic interventions which are not requested or desired by the patient or whose consequences and implications he does not fully understand. The question is not whether a given form of psychotherapy is promising but whether the psychotherapist has the right to subject nonconsenting adults to the procedure. Cognizant of this problem, the United States Public Health Service requires all investigators whose scientific work is supported by grants to obtain a signed consent statement from subjects or patients participating in research, and insists upon appropriate administrative supervision by universities and institutions with which investigators are affiliated. These regulations go some distance in dealing with the problem, but in the final analysis the responsibility rests with the individual investigator. Research and therapy are not identical, but very frequently research projects have therapeutic intent, and in the area of psychotherapy research therapeutic implications are almost always present. Where the research or the therapy requires the participation of patients, the criterion is not the *intent* of the investigator— the therapist or investigator may be extremely well intentioned, and even if he is not, it is possible to rationalize a procedure in terms of therapy or the advancement of knowledge—but the decision of the subject as to whether he wants to be "helped."

To illustrate: A state hospital institutes a program of behavior modification under the direction of a psychologist. A catatonic patient, a young woman who, according to the hospital's records, has been virtually mute for several years is confronted with a psychologist who operates on the working hypothesis that behavior can be effectively modified if one can control its consequences. Accordingly, the patient is informed that the psychologist will be present at mealtimes and that she will receive a given item of food on the menu if she asks for it in intelligible language; conversely, if she remains mute, she will go hungry. It is not specified whether the treatment will be continued indefinitely if the patient refuses to cooperate, but as far as she knows she may starve. The situation having been defined in this way, the patient may to some extent modify her catatonic behavior and begin to utter words, whereupon the psychologist will "reward" her by saying, "That was very good, Mary." The procedure is continued and the patient may increase her verbal output, which may be considered an improvement.

Is this form of therapy justifiable? The behavior therapist asserts that it is, on the grounds that the patient is being helped to abandon her stuporous state and to become more socialized. Whether the treatment will enable her to leave the hospital to lead a more or less normal life in the community is uncertain, but objectively she is using words more frequently than she was before.

It has been argued by some authors (Szasz, 1967) that this form of therapy constitutes an infringement of the patient's human rights. Unless one is willing to entertain the unlikely hypothesis that the patient's bizarre behavior is due to organic brain damage or impairment of the nervous system, it presumably has its roots in the patient's interpersonal experience. The behavior therapist is not interested in antecedents and considers them irrelevant to the problem at hand. The dynamic psychologist would hold that there are reasons for the patient's behavior. The reasons may not be clear to the observer, but if they were, one would not characterize the patient's behavior as "crazy" or "psychotic." This is a scientific problem. From the therapeutic standpoint one must ask: Does the patient have a right to engage in behavior which the psychopathologist may characterize as catatonic? In a free society, the answer must be Yes. Does society, or a psychotherapist, have the right to modify this behavior against the patient's wishes through coercive means? The answer to this question must be No.

The justification invoked by the behavior therapist is based on the same assumptions as those cited by psychiatrists for performing lobotomies or subjecting patients to electroconvulsive therapy: (1) The patient has lost control over his behavior and fails to discharge responsibilities demanded of adult citizens in society; and, (2) since the patient is psychotic, he does not know what is in his best interest, but the mental health professionals supposedly do; consequently, they have the right to decide what shall be done with the patient and how he shall be treated as a "sick" individual.

Society has the right to punish citizens who violate laws, and it may be forced to take care of persons who fail to earn a living, neglect parental responsibilities, or become helpless for a variety of reasons. But society does not have the right to perform therapy on these persons, change their behavior, or influence them by physical, chemical, or psychological means to behave in ways which are more socially acceptable, less deviant, or less troublesome.

In the example under discussion, a psychotherapist as an expert and as a concerned fellow human being may meet with the patient over a period of time, try to win her confidence, and if he is successful in this endeavor may help her understand the reasons for her actions and behavior. If as a result of this relationship the patient changes her behavior, well and good. She may learn that, contrary to earlier experiences, not all human beings are cruel, exploitative, and vicious, and she may see the "error of her ways." She may also come to feel that other ways of interacting may be more beneficial and more conducive to her well-being. But no theory of psychotherapy and no mandate by society justifies coercive measures to change human behavior; no matter how well-intentioned these efforts may be. For, once the basic right "to be let alone" is invaded, the state or its agents can similarly justify changing the behavior of any individual whose behavior is judged deviant, troublesome, or obnoxious. The point is that mental health is inextricably intertwined with moral judgments of good and evil, which are subject to arbitrary definitions.

From the preceding discussion it becomes clear that psychotherapy with patients who are forced to undergo "treatment" by their families, employers, a court of law, or by a mental hospital is fraught with serious ethical problems, quite apart from technical difficulties. It is also clear that under such circumstances the psychotherapist cannot function as the patient's agent.

It can be readily agreed that the psychotherapist is obligated to work in the patient's best interest. But what constitutes the patient's best interest? If the patient is suffering from phobic or depressive symptoms for which he seeks relief, and which may be directly attacked by some therapists, there are no serious dilemmas. Matters become more complicated when a timid patient, as a result of psychotherapy, begins to assert himself, say, vis-à-vis his spouse. Not infrequently, members of the patient's family, even though they may sympathize with his neurotic suffering, are quite content to see him remain as he is. (Despite his conscious desire for change, the patient, too, is committed to the status quo.) A domineering spouse will greatly prefer a submissive partner who satisfies some of her own neurotic needs. Thus, as soon as the patient "improves," an overt struggle may ensue within the marriage, and the wife may blame the therapist for aiding and abetting the patient's assertive behavior. Most people would feel that the therapist's responsibility is to the patient, not his wife. Furthermore, if the therapist confines his activity to helping the patient understand the *reasons* for his passivity without suggesting or implying how the patient should conduct himself, he remains true to his role. The dividing line between analyzing and suggesting modes of behavior, however, is a thin one, and the therapist has to steer a careful course. And we must not underestimate the patient's continual (and typically unconscious) efforts to wrest advice from the therapist. These maneuvers may take exceedingly subtle, but nonetheless insidious forms.

In some forms of psychotherapy (e.g., Albert Ellis's rational-emotive therapy), the therapist may openly advocate assertiveness, which then becomes a therapeutic goal or value. That is, he proceeds on the assumption that assertiveness on the part of a male adult in our society is preferable to submissiveness. If the patient agrees and acts accordingly, there may be no problem provided he understands that the responsibility for his actions and their consequences rests with him, not the therapist. This issue does not revolve around the merits of assertiveness as a mental health value; rather I am trying to show that (1) it is exceedingly difficult if not impossible for the therapist to maintain a completely neutral stance (which may not even be desirable); and (2) that his therapeutic operations almost inevitably become geared to goals which entail moral judgments about human conduct. According to Freud's view, the neurotic patient is like a prisoner who is chained by his symptoms and neurotic conflicts. The therapist, through his analytic efforts, frees the patient from his shackles, whereupon he is free to act freely, rationally, and responsibly. As an ideal, this conception is praiseworthy. In practice, the therapist cannot avoid advocating values which are implicit in our culture; conversely, therapy becomes effective when the patient accepts or identifies with these values, making them his own (Rosenthal, 1955). In sum, psychotherapy cannot be value free, and the values are moral judgments of good or evil.

A word should be said about situations in which the patient's behavior or values are at variance with those of the therapist or society. Suppose the patient engages in some form of sexual behavior considered deviant by society. He may be an exhibitionist, voyeur, or homosexual. Society condemns these behaviors, even where they do not entail harm to others and may constitute only a nuisance, and offenders may be punished by imprisonment, although there is now a growing tendency to view these behaviors as symptoms of an illness. If the patient himself is in conflict over his conduct and seeks therapy for the purpose of modifying it, the therapist simply proceeds with his work. It is interesting to note that in the sexual sphere, in contrast to attitudes common in Freud's nineteenth century Vienna, greater tolerance has gradually developed. This is less true in other areas of human conduct.

A patient, for example, may be a psychopath, partly defined as a person who violates the social code without experiencing marked anxiety or guilt. He may write bad checks, exploit others in various ways, or behave irresponsibly. Society as well as numerous psychotherapists (Strupp, 1960) respond with anger, hostility, and rejection to such patients. If the patient disapproves of himself and seeks psychotherapeutic help, a therapist may be able to set aside his personal feelings and deal with the "problem" relatively objectively. If he cannot honestly do that, he should not undertake to work with such a patient. Nor should he try to "reform" him. The situation is complicated because a therapist may not be clear about his own attitudes and motives.

Finally, there is the relatively rare occurrence when a therapist has serious reason to believe that the patient is on the verge of doing serious harm to himself or others; that is, he may contemplate suicide or murder. What is the therapist's responsibility? Can he afford to continue in the role of the professional helper who treats the patient's reports about feelings, motivations, and actions as "associations" or "data" which have neither a positive nor a negative valence? Should he inform the patient that he is abdicating the therapeutic role, advise him to seek hospitalization, or inform him that he will notify the police? Does the law require the therapist as a citizen to prevent an impending crime? If he fails to take action, he may become an accessory to a crime. If he reacts to the patient's revelations by informing the police, he has forfeited the patient's trust and the therapeutic relationship has come to an end. Threats by a patient are often a way to test the therapist's trustworthiness, to provoke him, or to create greater closeness. Thus they become an important part of the therapeutic problem and must be dealt with as such.

Clearly, there are no easy answers to the questions raised in this chapter. Our purpose has been to highlight some of the thorny problems which the psychotherapist frequently faces in his work and the challenges with which patients confront him. Furthermore, it is evident that psychotherapy, even when it is concerned with ostensibly minor adjustment problems, always represents a serious intervention in another person's life which should never be undertaken lightly. It requires intensive and prolonged training and careful supervision by experts. Since it deals with important human problems, it presupposes a keen sense of responsibility, firm commitment to the patient, and a thorough grasp of moral and ethical issues on the part of the therapist. Such attitudes are not acquired in the laboratory or in the library; rather, they are the product of sustained training, experience, and supervision.

Suggested Readings

FRANK, J. D. *Persuasion and healing: A comparative study of psychotherapy*. Baltimore: Johns Hopkins, 1961.

Szasz, T. S.   *Law, liberty and psychiatry.* New York: Macmillan, 1963.

Szasz, T. S.   *The ethics of psychoanalysis.* New York: Basic Books, 1965.

Szasz, T. S.   Behavior therapy and psychoanalysis. *Medical Opinion and Review,* 1967, 3, 24–29.

APPENDIX B

The Psychotherapy Professions and Problems of Training

Several professions engage in the practice of psychotherapy and behavior modification, and there is a good deal of overlap in the professional activities. The lines of demarcation are often not very clear, and in general the professions are identifiable more clearly in terms of the training their members receive than the professional activities. Nevertheless, each profession has its area of specialization, and it is important to keep these apart.

The *psychiatrist* is always medically trained and holds the M.D. degree. In addition to basic training in medicine, he must complete a residency in psychiatry (usually three to four years). During his residency he acquires competence in treating a variety of mental and emotional disorders in inpatients and outpatients, adults and children, and he may become involved in clinical research, community mental health, and similar areas of interest. Psychiatry is a medical specialty, and the psychiatrist rightly considers himself first and foremost a physician. As a physician he is legally entitled to prescribe drugs, perform physical examinations, and carry out somatic treatment (e.g., electroconvulsive therapy, insulin therapy). He may also use psychological techniques of all kinds and combine psychotherapy with drug therapy.

Psychiatrists are uniquely qualified to treat the whole range of emotional and mental disorders, particularly serious disturbances requiring hospitalization, but many psychiatrists specialize in psychotherapy and prescribe drugs very sparingly. In practice, however, many psychiatrists do not perform physical examinations and refer patients to other medical specialists for somatic treatment, even if the disorder (e.g., peptic ulcer, asthma) is judged to have a psychogenic basis. Because of their medical background they may at times be more sensitive to intercurrent physical ailments in their patients and refer them to the appropriate specialist. These skills are also valuable in diagnosis, but here the psychiatrist typically consults with other specialists in medicine (such as the neurologist, internist, etc.), the clinical psychologist, and the psychiatric social worker. In clinics and hospitals, collaboration between the psychiatrist, clinical psychologist, and psychiatric social worker is routine. These professions are often referred to as the "psychiatric team." This cooperation is notably effective in arriving at a diagnostic formulation; if the recommended treatment is psychotherapy, any member of the team may assume the primary responsibility.

Psychotherapy and behavior modification, as we have seen, are radically different from any form of medical treatment, and the psychiatrist, to the extent that he engages in these activities, cannot be said to practice medicine. The medical patient is truly the passive recipient of a treatment, and the physician is unquestionably the authority in charge. As previously stated, in psychotherapy, the roles of the participants bear only a vague resemblance to his model, and the terms "patient" and "doctor" are really misnomers which should be abandoned. Unfortunately, their use is deeply entrenched, and the English language has no good substitutes. The terms "client" and "therapist" have often been substituted but are not entirely satisfactory either. The medical patient's attitude toward an injection of penicillin has little bearing on the pharmacological action of the drug,° and the success of an appendectomy is not significantly determined by the patient's feelings about the surgical procedure. In psychotherapy, of course, the patient's feelings, attitudes, and motivation are central. There are also important differences between the therapist's and the physician's stance vis-à-vis a patient.

Acrimonious debates have marred relations between psychiatry and other professions concerned with psychotherapy. Regrettably, considerations of power and prestige seem to have influenced the problem to a greater extent than the interest of the patient, but fortunately the bitterness of the struggle seems to be waning. The major contention of organized psychiatry has been that psychotherapy is a form of *medical* treatment and its practice therefore should be reserved to physicians. Against this it has been argued that by this narrow definition any psychological technique designed to modify the feelings, attitudes, and behavior of another person (including vocational counseling, pastoral counseling, marital counseling, and many others) would fall under the rubric of a medical specialty. The remarkable growth of

° Placebo effects, however, are almost always present.

the nonmedical professions practicing psychotherapy and the passage of licensing or certification laws in many states document that society is taking a more liberal view.

The *psychoanalyst* specializes in the application of psychological techniques which, for the most part, are based on the teachings of Sigmund Freud and his followers. "Classical" or "orthodox" psychoanalysis is aimed at a large-scale reorganization of the patient's personality and typically requires several years of intensive work. The patient is seen four to five hours per week, reclines on a couch (although this is not an absolute requirement), and is instructed to follow the "fundamental rule" of free association. Analysis of resistances and transference feelings by means of interpretations is the majc : technique.

The training of the psychoanalyst includes personal analysis (previously called didactic analysis but now almost indistinguishable from a therapeutic analysis), extensive study of psychoanalytic theory and technique, and careful supervision of several cases (so-called control analyses). Psychoanalysts unquestionably receive the most systematic and comprehensive training offered to psychotherapists.

Historically, the practice of psychoanalysis did not call for background training in medicine or psychiatry, and in fact many notable psychoanalysts came from other fields. Such therapists were (misleadingly) called *lay analysts,* now an obsolete term. Freud felt very strongly that psychoanalysis was a branch of psychology, not of medicine or psychiatry.

Contrary to his views, however, psychoanalysis in this country became allied with medicine, and the American Psychoanalytic Association established the rule that all psychoanalysts must have completed full psychiatric training in addition to specialized training in psychoanalysis. Therefore, most American psychoanalysts today are psychiatrists although the term "psychoanalyst" has no legal status comparable to psychiatrist. Numerous splinter groups in this country also train analysts, and the background training of their members may be in some nonmedical area. All psychoanalytic training is carried out by special institutes rather than by universities. For various reasons, including the relative scarcity of patients considered ideally suited for orthodox analysis, psychoanalysts often practice so-called analytically oriented psychotherapy. This form of therapy is based on psychoanalytic principles, but various modifications are introduced in the classical technique. Therapists engaged in this form of therapy should not strictly be called psychoanalysts.

A considerable amount of psychotherapy today is administered by therapists whose training has been in *clinical psychology*. The clinical psychologist usually has earned the Ph.D. degree and in addition to training in research design and methodology has undertaken specialized training in clinical psychology. Clinical psychology became a prominent branch of psychology following World War II, and a steadily increasing number of students have been trained since that time. Clinical psychology grew out of academic psychology with which it has continued to maintain close ties. The doctoral degree in clinical psychology requires a minimum of three to four years graduate training (beyond the bachelor degree) in a university program accredited by the American Psychological Association plus a year of internship training in a mental hospital or clinic. In addition, clinical psychologists often complete one to two years of postdoctoral training. Beyond a number of courses in various branches of academic psychology, the clinical psychologist receives training and supervised experience in psychodiagnosis and psychotherapy. The term "behavior modification" was introduced by psychologists and denotes the emergence of several new forms of psychotherapy based on learning principles. Psychotherapists whose background training has been in clinical psychology are working extensively with adults, children, and families. They may specialize in individual therapy, group therapy, and numerous variants. Frequently they are engaged in group or clinic practice, although some are private practitioners. While standards of training have emerged only in the recent past, many clinical psychologists are highly trained psychotherapists. Five years of experience beyond the Ph.D. degree and passing of a set of examinations qualify the clinical psychologist for Diplomate status, which is conferred by the American Board of Professional Psychology (ABPP). By far the largest amount of research in psychotherapy and behavior modification is contributed by psychologists.

A sizable amount of psychotherapy is being carried out by *psychiatric social workers* who, with clinical psychologists, form the largest group of nonmedical psychotherapists. Psychiatric social workers typically complete two years of graduate training in which supervised field training at a mental hygiene clinic or hospital plays a prominent part. Traditionally, social workers have been concerned with the social setting in which the patient functions. With the growing emphasis upon viewing the patient's emotional problems in the context of his family situation and the social setting, the psychiatric social worker is uniquely equipped to meet this need. Training in research is a relatively recent facet of psychiatric social work.

Psychotherapy is also practiced by pastoral counselors, marital counselors, and several other professional groups whose training may be in diverse fields.

TOWARD UNIFIED TRAINING IN PSYCHOTHERAPY

As we have seen, training in psychotherapy forms part of the curriculum of several professional groups, but these programs also have other objectives, some of which are only indirectly related to the practice of psychotherapy. For example: In the case of the psychiatrist, medical training involves courses in anatomy, biochemistry, and many other subjects which have little relevance to his activities as a psychiatrist; and the clinical psychologist's academic training includes courses in perception, physiological psychology, and other areas which are not germane. If the practice of psychotherapy requires special skills, why not develop a training program geared specifically to the development of these skills? In this way it might be possible to combine the best aspects of different training programs, eliminate detours and duplications, and train a practitioner in a much shorter period of time. But what should such a curriculum contain? Should there be a new professional school? How can inevitable conflicts with existing training programs be resolved? What are the criteria for a well-trained psychotherapist?

With the advent of psychoanalysis and the need for structured training programs to train professional therapists, Freud and his collaborators decided in favor of special training institutes. This development was based on the realization that existing academic programs, both in medicine and academic psychology, were unsuitable; besides, both groups had shown marked hostility toward psychoanalysis. While attitudes have undergone some change, academic programs have not become any more appropriate. To graft training in psychotherapy on existing university curricula seemed to add unnecessarily to the length of training, in addition to being wasteful for other reasons. Arguing from this vantage point, Kubie (1954) proposed a new training program which would combine courses in basic biological science with relevant instruction in the social sciences. In addition, of course, the student would receive supervised experience in conducting psychotherapy. Finally, some form of personal therapy, to give the student first-hand experience with the forces and processes he is called upon to work with in others, has traditionally been considered a prime ingredient in psychotherapeutic training. Kubie's proposal was never implemented, nor have subsequent interdisciplinary conferences been able to bring about radical revisions. Part of the problem may stem from a reluctance of the various disciplines to relinquish some of their vested interests and power.

Since psychotherapy is not a unified discipline, there can hardly be a single ideal training program. A person practicing behavior therapy is poles apart from a psychoanalyst—in techniques, theoretical convictions, therapeutic goals, and temperament; and the same may be said about other groups. Nevertheless, it may be possible to specify a few salient requirements a psychotherapist should meet:

1. He should have a measure of emotional maturity and be aware of those aspects of his personality which are likely to create difficulties in his interaction with patients. The author is convinced that an awareness of the therapist's "stimulus value" can best be acquired through personal therapy, which is very likely the most important single learning experience the young therapist can undergo. Many personal qualities have been mentioned as highly desirable (Holt & Luborsky, 1958), but the therapist cannot be at once a paragon of virtue, an intellectual giant, a supremely sensitive human being, and a sage. Indeed, there is evidence that individuals who are distinctly imperfect can do a creditable job as a psychotherapist. It also appears that people who have struggled with personal difficulties may be better candidates than bland, normal individuals who have had little direct experience with anxiety and distress.

2. He should have a fair grounding in the biological and social sciences. Familiarity with different cultures, religions, and mythologies is probably more important than mathematical or quantitative skills. He should be thoroughly familiar with psychopathology, and extensive

experience with a wide range of disordered persons in mental hospitals and clinics is equally important. Knowledge of important contributions to the world literature adds another dimension of cultural breadth. Academic training programs in psychiatry, psychology, and social work tend to foster narrow specialization, which is undesirable in a psychotherapist, who must deal with the gamut of human experience.

3. While study of various theories of personality, psychopathology, and psychotherapy is important, the practice of psychotherapy is essentially an art and a skill which can only be acquired through practice and prolonged supervision by a seasoned expert. The master-apprentice relationship unquestionably remains the best model. Psychotherapy training requires dedication, discipline, and hard work; no one should have the illusion that it can be otherwise. Since many problems with which the psychotherapist must deal are the result of faulty learning over a long period of time, it is most unlikely that the unlearning of old patterns and the learning of more adaptive ones can be accomplished by waving a magic wand or other miracular means:

> Historical perspective suggests that in some future epoch of a still more enlightened culture we shall have accepted finally and unreservedly the inescapable need to treat by teaching, the inescapable truth that deprivations of love are not remediable by offers of capsules. We shall have learned that faulty logic is not the result solely of chemical imbalance and that a long history of maladaptive behavior requires a protracted period of instruction in hygienic thinking coupled with *personal* reward for that thinking and its attendant changes in behavior [Schofield, 1964, p. 84].

The above account clearly suggests that psychotherapists should have extensive and intensive training. However, since research on the outcome of psychotherapy has not yet provided unequivocal answers, we are equally uncertain about the qualifications of a good therapist and the kind of training he should undergo. Under the circumstances authoritative recommendations are certainly premature. The question may also be raised whether persons with less than "full training" can function as effective psychotherapists.

This issue has become particularly urgent since none of the major disciplines, singly or in combination, can possibly meet the growing need for therapeutic services. Addressing itself to this issue, the Joint Commission on Mental Illness and Health recommended: "In the absence of fully trained psychiatrists, clinical psychologists, psychiatric social workers, and psychiatric nurses, [preventive] counseling should be done by persons with some psychological orientation and mental health training and access to expert consultation as needed."

Some evidence supporting the feasibility of limited training has come from a pilot study carried out by Rioch et al. (1963), to which reference has been made earlier (Chapter 5). Truax and Carkhuff (1967) have shown that such qualities as empathy and warmth can be enhanced through systematic training. Schofield (1964) has argued for a proper appreciation of "therapeutic conversation," which probably can be provided by persons other than highly trained psychotherapists and offers alternatives to the great social need which cannot be met in other ways (see also Chapter 5).

Ultimately, of course, it is essential to achieve greater specificity concerning the nature of the task to be performed by the psychotherapist and the objectives to be reached. There is reasonable agreement concerning the skills a surgeon, a pianist, or a craftsman must possess. Uncertainties about the proper training of psychotherapists underscore the diffuseness of aims and the techniques needed to achieve them.

Suggested Readings

BLANK, L., & DAVID, H. P. (Eds.)   *Sourcebook for training in clinical psychology.* New York: Springer, 1964.

JOINT COMMISSION ON MENTAL ILLNESS AND HEALTH.   *Action for mental health.* New York: Basic Books, 1961.

KUBIE, L. S.   The pros and cons of a new profession: A doctorate in medical psychology. *Texas Reports on Biology and Medicine* 1954, **12**, 692–737.

LUBIN, B., & LEVITT, E. E. (Eds.)   *The clinical psychologist: Background, roles, and functions.* Chicago: Aldine, 1967.

WOLMAN, B. B. (Ed.)   *Handbook of clinical psychology.* New York: McGraw-Hill, 1965.

REFERENCES

ALEXANDER, F. *Five Year report of the Chicago Institute for Psycho-analysis, 1932–1937.*

ALLPORT, G. W. *Becoming.* New Haven, Conn.: Yale, 1955.

ARGYRIS, C. *Interpersonal competence and organizational effectiveness.* Chicago: Irwin-Dorsey, 1962.

ASHBY, J. D., FORD, D. H., GUERNEY, B. G., JR., & GUERNEY, L. F. Effects on clients of a reflective and a leading type of psychotherapy. *Psychological Monographs,* 1957, **71** (Whole No. 453).

AUERBACH, A. H., & LUBORSKY, L. Accuracy of judgments of psychotherapy and the nature of the "good hour." In J. M. Shlien et. al. (Eds.), *Research in psychotherapy,* Vol. 3. Washington, D.C.: American Psychological Association, 1968. Pp. 155–168.

AULD, F., JR., & MURRAY, E. J. Content-analysis studies of psychotherapy. *Psychological Bulletin,* 1955, **52,** 377–395.

AULD, F., JR., & MYERS, J. K. Contributions to a theory for selecting psychotherapy patients. *Journal of Clinical Psychology,* 1954, **10,** 56–60.

BACHRACH, A. J., ERWIN, W. J., & MOHR, J. P. The control of eating behavior in an anorexic by operant conditioning techniques. In L. P. Ullmann & L. Krasner (Eds.), *Case studies in behavior modification.* New York: Holt, 1965. Pp. 153–163.

BAKAN, D. *On method.* San Francisco: Jossey-Bass, 1967.

BANDURA, A. Psychotherapist's anxiety level, self-insight, and psychotherapeutic competence. *Journal of Abnormal and Social Psychology,* 1956, **52,** 333–337.

BANDURA, A. Behavioral modification through modeling procedures. In L. Krasner & L. P. Ullmann (Eds.), *Research in behavior modification.* New York: Holt, 1965. Pp. 310–340.

BANDURA, A. Influence of models: Reinforcement contingencies on the acquisition of imitative responses. *Journal of Personality and Social Psychology*, 1965, 1, 589–595.

BANDURA, A., LIPSHER, D., & MILLER, P. Psychotherapist's approach-avoidance reactions to patient's expressions of hostility. *Journal of Consulting Psychology*, 1960, 24, 1–8.

BAUM, O. E., FELZER, S. B., D'ZMURA, T. L., & SHUMAKER, E. Psychotherapy, dropouts and lower socioeconomic patients. *American Journal of Orthopsychiatry*, 1966, 36, 629–635.

BERELSON, B. *Content analysis in communication research*. Glencoe, Ill.: Free Press, 1952.

BERGIN, A. E. The evaluation of therapeutic outcomes. In A. E. Bergin & S. L. Garfield (Eds.), *Handbook of psychotherapy and behavior change: An empirical analysis*. New York: Wiley, 1970.

BERZON, B., & SOLOMON, L. N. Research frontier: The self-directed therapeutic group—three studies. *Journal of Counseling Psychology*, 1966, 13, 491–497.

BOHN, M. J., JR. Counselor behavior as a function of counselor dominance, counselor experience, and client types. *Journal of Counseling Psychology*, 1965, 12, 346–352.

BRADFORD, L. P., GIBB, J. R., & BENNE, K. D. *T group theory and laboratory method*. New York: Wiley, 1964.

BRADFORD, L. P., GIBB, J. R., & LIPPITT, G. L. Human relations training in three days. *Adult Leadership*, 1956, 4, 11–26.

BREGER, L., & MCGAUGH, J. L. Critique and reformulation of "learning-theory" approaches to psychotherapy and neurosis. *Psychological Bulletin*, 1965, 63, 338–358.

BREUER, J., & FREUD, S. *Studies on hysteria*. New York: Basic Books, 1957.

BUGENTAL, J. F. T. *The search for authenticity*. New York: Holt, 1965.

BUHLER, C. *Values in psychotherapy*. New York: Free Press of Glencoe, 1962.

CARKHUFF, R. R., & TRUAX, C. B. Lay mental health counseling. *Journal of Consulting Psychology*, 1965, 29, 426–431.

CARSON, R. C. A and B therapist "types:" A possible critical variable in psychotherapy. *Journal of Nervous and Mental Disease*, 1967, 144, 47–54.

CARTWRIGHT, R. D. Psychotherapeutic processes. In P. R. Farnsworth (Ed.), *Annual Review of Psychology.* Palo Alto, California: Annual Reviews, 1968. Pp. 387–416.

CARTWRIGHT, R. D., & VOGEL, J. L. A comparison of changes in psychoneurotic patients during matched periods of therapy and no therapy. *Journal of Consulting Psychology,* 1960, **24,** 121–127.

CHASSAN, J. B. *Research design in clinical psychology and psychiatry.* New York: Appleton-Century-Crofts 1967.

CHOMSKY, N. Review of B. F. Skinner, *Verbal behavior. Language,* 1959, **35,** 26–58.

CLEMES, S. R., & D'ANDREA, V. J. Patient's anxiety as a function of expectation and degree of initial interview ambiguity. *Journal of Consulting Psychology,* 1965, **29,** 397–404.

CUTLER, R. Countertransference effects in psychotherapy. *Journal of Consulting Psychology,* 1958, **22,** 349–356.

DEANE, W. N., & ANSBACHER, H. L. Attendant-patient commonality as a psychotherapeutic factor. *Journal of Individual Psychology,* 1962, **18,** 157–167.

EINSTEIN, A. Physics and reality. In C. Seelig (Ed.), *Ideas and opinions by Albert Einstein.* New York: Crown Publishers, 1954.

ELLIS, A. *Reason and emotion in psychotherapy.* New York: Lyle Stuart, 1962.

EYSENCK, H. J. The effects of psychotherapy: An evaluation. *Journal of Consulting Psychology,* 1952, **16,** 319–324.

EYSENCK, H. J. Learning theory and behavior therapy. *Journal of Mental Science,* 1959, **105,** 61–75.

EYSENCK, H. J. *Handbook of abnormal psychology.* New York: Basic Books, 1961.

FENICHEL, O. Statistischer Bericht über die therapeutische Tätigkeit 1920–1930. In *Zehn Jahre Berliner Psychoanalytisches Institut.* Vienna: Internationaler Psychoanalytischer Verlag, 1930. Pp. 13–19.

FIEDLER, F. E. The concept of an ideal therapeutic relationship. *Journal of Consulting Psychology,* 1950, **14,** 239–245. (b)

FIEDLER, F. E. A comparison of therapeutic relationships in psychoanalytic, non-directive, and Adlerian therapy. *Journal of Consulting Psychology,* 1950, **14,** 436–445. (a)

FORD, D. H., & URBAN, H. B. *Systems of psychotherapy.* New York: Wiley, 1963.

FRANK, J. D. Problems of control in psychotherapy as exemplified by the psychotherapy research project of the Phipps Psychiatric Clinic. In A. D. Rubinstein & M. B. Parloff (Eds.), *Research in psychotherapy*. Vol. 1. Washington, D.C.: American Psychological Association, 1959. Pp. 10–26.

FRANK, J. D. *Persuasion and healing: A comparative study of psychotherapy*. Baltimore: Johns Hopkins, 1961.

FREUD, A. The widening scope of indications for psychoanalysis. *Journal of American Psychoanalytic Association*, 1954, **2**, 607–620.

FREUD, S. Analysis terminable and interminable. In *Collected Papers*. Vol. V. London: Hogarth, 1952. Pp. 316–357.

FREUD, S. Lines of advance in psycho-analytic therapy. In J. Strachey (Ed.), *The complete psychological works of Sigmund Freud*. Vol. XVII. London: Hogarth, 1955. Pp. 157–168.

FREUD, S. The future prospects of psycho-analytic therapy. In J. Strachey (Ed.), *The complete psychological works of Sigmund Freud*. Vol. XI. London: Hogarth, 1957. Pp. 139–151.

FRIEDLANDER, F. A comparative study of consulting processes and group development. *Journal of Applied Behavioral Science*, 1968, **4**, 377–399.

GARDNER, G. G. The psychotherapeutic relationship. *Psychological Bulletin*, 1964, **61**, 426–437.

GELDER, M. G., Marks, I. M., & Wolff, H. H. Desensitization and psychotherapy in the treatment of phobic states: A controlled inquiry. *British Journal of Psychiatry*, 1967, **113**, 53–73.

GENDLIN, E. T. *Experiencing and the creation of meaning*. New York: Free Press of Glencoe, 1962.

GIBB, J. R. The effects of human relations training. In A. E. Bergin & S. Garfield (Eds.), *Handbook of psychotherapy and behavior change: An empirical analysis*. New York: Wiley, 1970.

GIBB, J. R., & GIBB, L. M. Emergency therapy: The TORI process in an emergent group. In G. M. Gazda (Ed.), *Innovations to group psychotherapy*. Springfield, Ill.: Thomas, 1968. Pp. 96–129.

GLOVER, E. *The technique of psychoanalysis* (Rev. ed.). New York: International Universities, 1958.

GOIN, M. K., YAMAMOTO, J., & SILVERMAN, J. Therapy congruent with class-linked expectations. *Archives of General Psychiatry*, 1965, **13**, 133–137.

GOLDSTEIN, A. P., HELLER, K., & SECHREST, L. B. *Psychotherapy and the psychology of behavior change.* New York: Wiley, 1966.

GOULD, R. E.   Dr. Strangeclass: Or, how I stopped worrying about the theory and began treating the blue-collar worker. *American Journal of Orthopsychiatry,* 1967, **37**, 78–86.

HARPER, R. A.   *Psychoanalysis and psychotherapy: 36 systems.* Englewood Cliffs, Prentice-Hall, 1959.

HEINE, R. W., & TROSMAN, H.   Initial expectations of the doctor-patient interaction as a factor in continuance in psychotherapy. *Psychiatry,* 1960, **23**, 275–278.

HELLER, K., & GOLDSTEIN, A. P.   Client dependency and therapist expectancy as relationship maintaining variables in psychotherapy. *Journal of Consulting Psychology,* 1961, **25**, 371–375.

HOEHN-SARIC, R., FRANK, J. D., IMBER, S. D., NASH, E. H., STONE, A. R., & BATTLE, C. C.   Systematic preparation of patients for psychotherapy-I. Effects on therapy behavior and outcome. *Journal of Psychiatric Research,* 1964, **2**, 267–281.

HOLLINGSHEAD, A. B., & REDLICH, F. C.   *Social class and mental illness.* New York: Wiley, 1958.

HOLT, R. R., & LUBORSKY, L.   *Personality patterns of psychiatrists: A study in selection techniques.* New York: Basic Books, 1958.

ISAACS, K. S., & HAGGARD, E. A.   Some methods used in the study of affect in psychotherapy. In L. A. Gottschalk & A. H. Auerbach (Eds.), *Methods of research in psychotherapy.* New York: Appleton-Century-Crofts, 1966. Pp. 226–239.

JOINT COMMISSION ON MENTAL ILLNESS AND HEALTH.   *Action for mental health.* New York: Basic Books, 1961.

JONES, E.   *Decennial report of the London Clinic of Psychoanalysis, 1926–1936.*

JONES, M. C.   A laboratory study of fear: The case of Peter. *Pedagogical Seminary,* 1924, **31**, 308–315.

KAPLAN, F.   Effects of anxiety and defense in a therapy-like situation. *Journal of Abnormal Psychology,* 1966, **71**, 449–458.

KEITH-SPIEGEL, P., & SPIEGEL, D.   Perceived helpfulness of others as a function of compatible intelligence levels. *Journal of Counseling Psychology,* 1967, **14**, 61–62.

KESSEL, L., & HYMAN, H. T.   The value of psychoanalysis as a therapeutic procedure. *Journal of the American Medical Association,* 1933, **101**, 1612–1615.

KNIGHT, R. P. Evaluation of the results of psychoanalytic therapy. *American Journal of Psychiatry*, 1941, **98**, 434–446.

KRASNER, L. The therapist as a social reinforcement machine. In H. H. Strupp & L. Luborsky (Eds.), *Research in psychotherapy*. Vol. 2. Washington, D. C.: American Psychological Association, 1962. Pp. 61–94.

KRASNER, L. Verbal conditioning and psychotherapy. In L. Krasner & L. P. Ullmann (Eds.), *Research in behavior modification*. New York: Holt, 1965. Pp. 211–228.

KUBIE, L. S. The pros and cons of a new profession: A doctorate in medical psychology. *Texas Reports on Biology and Medicine*, 1954, **12**, 692–737.

LANG, P. J., & MELAMED, B. G. Avoidance conditioning therapy of an infant with chronic ruminative vomiting. *Journal of Abnormal Psychology*, 1969, **74**, 1–8.

LENNARD, H. L., & BERNSTEIN, A. *The anatomy of psychotherapy*. New York: Columbia, 1960.

LEVITT, E. Psychotherapy research and the expectation-reality discrepancy. *Psychotherapy*, 1966, **3**, 163–166.

LOHRENZ, J. G., HUNTER, R. C., & SCHWARTZMAN, A. E. Factors relevant to positive psychotherapeutic responses in university students. *Canadian Psychiatric Association Journal*, 1966, **11**, 38–42.

LOVAAS, O. I., SCHAEFFER, B., & SIMMONS, J. Q. Building social behavior in autistic children by use of electric shock. *Journal of Experimental Research in Personality*, 1965, **1**, 99–109.

LUBORSKY, L. A note on Eysenck's article, "The effects of psychotherapy: An evaluation." *British Journal of Psychology*, 1954, **45**, 129–131.

LUBORSKY, L. Psychotherapy. In P. R. Farnsworth & Q. McNemar (Eds.), *Annual Review of Psychology*. Palo Alto, California: Annual Reviews, 1959. Pp. 317–344.

MARSDEN, G. Content-analysis studies of therapeutic interviews: 1954–1964. *Psychological Bulletin*, 1965, **63**, 298–319.

MARSDEN, G. Content analysis studies of psychotherapy. In A. E. Bergin & S. L. Garfield (Eds.), *Handbook of psychotherapy and behavior change: An empirical analysis*. New York: Wiley, 1970.

MASSIMO, J. L., & SHORE, M. F. The effectiveness of a comprehensive, vocationally oriented psychotherapeutic program for adolescent delinquent boys. *American Journal of Orthopsychiatry*, 1963, **33**, 634–642.

MATARAZZO, J. D., WIENS, A. N., & SASLOW, G. Studies in interview speech behavior. In L. Krasner & L. P. Ullmann (Eds.), *Research in behavior modification.* New York: Holt, 1965. Pp. 179–210.

MAY, R., ANGEL, E., & ELLENBERGER, H. F. (Eds.) *Existence: A new dimension in psychiatry and psychology.* New York: Basic Books, 1958.

MCNAIR, D. M., CALLAHAN, D. M., & LORR, M. Therapist "type" and patient response to psychotherapy. *Journal of Consulting Psychology*, 1962, **26**, 425–429.

MCNAIR, D. M., LORR, M., & CALLAHAN, D. M. Patient and therapist influences on quitting psychotherapy. *Journal of Consulting Psychology*, 1963, **27**, 10–17.

MILES, M. B. Changes during and following laboratory training: A clinical-experimental study. *Journal of Applied Behavioral Science*, 1965, **1**, 215–242.

NASH, E. H., HOEHN-SARIC, R., BATTLE, C. C., STONE, A. R., IMBER, S. D., & FRANK, J. D. Systematic preparation of patients for short-term psychotherapy. II. Relation to characteristics of patient, therapist, and the psychotherapeutic process. *Journal of Nervous and Mental Disease*, 1965, **140**, 374–383.

ORLINSKY, D. E., & HOWARD, K. I. The good therapy hour: Experiential correlates of patients' and therapists' evaluations of therapy sessions. *Archives of General Psychiatry*, 1967, **16**, 621–632.

OTTO, H. A., & MANN, J. *Ways of growth: Approaches to exploring awareness.* New York: Grossman, 1968.

OVERALL, B., & ARONSON, H. Expectations of psychotherapy in patients of lower socio-economic class. *American Journal of Orthopsychiatry*, 1963, **33**, 421–430.

PAUL, G. *Insight vs. desensitization in psychotherapy.* Stanford, Calif.: Stanford, 1966.

PITTENGER, R. E., HOCKETT, C. F., & DANEHY, J. J. *The first five minutes.* Ithaca, N. Y.: Paul Martineau, 1960.

POSER, E. The effects of therapists' training on group therapeutic outcome. *Journal of Consulting Psychology*, 1966, **30**, 283–289.

RAUSH, H. L., & BORDIN, E. S. Warmth in personality development and in psychotherapy. *Psychiatry*, 1957, **20**, 351–363.

RICE, L. N.   Therapist's style of participation and case outcome. *Journal of Consulting Psychology,* 1965, **29,** 155–160.

RICE, L. N., & WAGSTAFF, A. K.   Client voice quality and expressive style as indexes of productive psychotherapy. *Journal of Consulting Psychology,* 1967, **31,** 557–563.

RIESSMAN, F., COHEN, J., & PEARL, A.   *Mental health of the poor.* New York: Free Press, 1964.

RIOCH, M. J., ELKES, C., FLINT, A., USDANSKY, B. S., NEWMAN, R. G., & SILBER, E.   National Institute of Mental Health pilot study in training mental health counselors. *American Journal of Orthopsychiatry,* 1963, **33,** 678–689.

ROGERS, C. R.   *Client-centered therapy.* Boston: Houghton Mifflin, 1951.

ROGERS, C. R.   The necessary and sufficient conditions of therapeutic personality change. *Journal of Consulting Psychology,* 1957, **21,** 95–103.

ROGERS, C. R.   A tentative scale for the measurement of process in psychotherapy. In E. A. Rubinstein & M. B. Parloff (Eds.), *Research in psychotherapy.* Vol. 1. Washington, D. C.: American Psychological Association, 1959. Pp. 96–107.

ROGERS, C. R.   *On becoming a person.* Boston: Houghton Mifflin, 1961.

ROGERS, C. R.   Client-centered psychotherapy. In A. M. Freedman & H. I. Kaplan (Eds.), *Comprehensive textbook of psychiatry.* Baltimore: Williams & Wilkins, 1967. Pp. 1225–1228.

ROGERS, C. R., & DYMOND, R. F.   *Psychotherapy and personality change.* Chicago: University of Chicago, 1954.

ROGERS, C. R., GENDLIN, E. T., KIESLER, D. J., & TRUAX, C. B.   *The therapeutic relationship and its impact.* Madison: University of Wisconsin, 1967.

ROSENTHAL, D.   Changes in some moral values following psychotherapy. *Journal of Consulting Psychology,* 1955, **19,** 431–436.

ROSENZWEIG, S.   A transvaluation of psychotherapy: A reply to Hans Eysenck. *Journal of Abnormal and Social Psychology,* 1954, **49,** 298–304.

RUBINSTEIN, E. A., & PARLOFF, M. B. (Eds.)   *Research in psychotherapy.* Vol. 1. Washington, D. C.: American Psychological Association, 1959.

Russell, B. *Human knowledge: Its scope and limits.* New York: Simon and Schuster, 1948.

Sandifer, M. G., Hordern, A., Timbury, G. C., & Green, L. M. Psychiatric diagnosis: A comparative study in North Carolina, London, and Glasgow. *British Journal of Psychiatry,* 1968, **114,** 1–9.

Schein, E. H., & Bennis, W. G. *Personal and organizational change through group methods.* New York: Wiley, 1965.

Schofield, W. *Psychotherapy: The purchase of friendship.* Englewood Cliffs, N. J.: Prentice-Hall, 1964.

Shlien, J. M., Hunt, H. F., Matarazzo, J. D., and Savage, C. (Eds.) *Research in psychotherapy.* Vol. 3. Washington, D. C.: American Psychological Association, 1968.

Shlien, J. M., Mosak, H. H., & Dreikurs, R. Effects of time limits: A comparison of client-centered and Adlerian psychotherapy. *American Psychologist,* 1960, **15,** 415. (Abstract)

Sifneos, P. E. Two different kinds of psychotherapy of short duration. *American Journal of Psychiatry,* 1967, **123,** 1069–1074.

Slack, C. W. Experimenter-subject psychotherapy: A new method of introducing intensive office treatment for unreachable cases. *Mental Hygiene,* 1960, 44, 238–256.

Stephens, J. H., & Astrup, C. Treatment outcome in "process" and "nonprocess" schizophrenics treated by "A" and "B" types of therapist. *Journal of Nervous and Mental Disease,* 1965, **140,** 449–456.

Stoler, N. Client likability: A variable in the study of psychotherapy. *Journal of Consulting Psychology,* 1963, **27,** 175–178.

Stoller, F. H. Marathon group therapy. In G. M. Gazda (Ed.), *Innovations to group psychotherapy.* Springfield, Ill.: Thomas, 1968. Pp. 42–95.

Stone, A. R., Frank, J. D., Nash, E. H., & Imber, S. D. An intensive five-year follow-up study of treated psychiatric outpatients. *Journal of Nervous and Mental Disease,* 1961, **133,** 410–422.

Strupp, H. H. Psychotherapeutic technique, professional affiliation, and experience level. *Journal of Consulting Psychology,* 1955, **19,** 97–102.

Strupp, H. H. The psychotherapist's contribution to the treatment process. *Behavioral Science,* 1958, 3, 34–67.

Strupp, H. H. *Psychotherapists in action.* New York: Grune and Stratton, 1960.

STRUPP, H. H.   Patient-doctor relationships: The psychotherapist in the therapeutic process. In A. J. Bachrach (Ed.), *Experimental foundations of clinical psychology*. New York: Basic Books, 1962. Pp. 576–615.

STRUPP, H. H.   The outcome problem in psychotherapy revisited. *Psychotherapy*, 1963, 1, 1–13.

STRUPP, H. H., & BERGIN, A. E.   *Research in individual psychotherapy: A bibliography*. Chevy Chase, Md.: National Clearinghouse for Mental Health Information, 1969.

STRUPP, H. H., & BERGIN, A. E.   Some empirical and conceptual bases for coordinated research in psychotherapy: A critical review of issues, trends, and evidence. *International Journal of Psychiatry*, 1969, 7, 18–90.

STRUPP, H. H., CHASSAN, J. B., & EWING, J. A.   Toward the longitudinal study of the psychotherapeutic process. In L. A. Gottschalk & A. H. Auerbach (Eds.), *Methods of research in psychotherapy*. New York: Appleton-Century-Crofts, 1966. Pp. 361–400.

STRUPP, H. H., FOX, R. E., & LESSLER, K.   *Patients view their psychotherapy*. Baltimore: Johns Hopkins, 1969.

STRUPP, H. H., & LUBORSKY, L. (Eds.)   *Research in psychotherapy*. Vol. 2. Washington, D. C.: American Psychological Association, 1962.

STRUPP, H. H., & WALLACH, M. S.   A further study of psychiatrists' responses in quasi-therapy situations. *Behavioral Science*, 1965, 10, 113–134.

STRUPP, H. H., & WILLIAMS, J. V.   Some determinants of clinical evaluations of different psychiatrists. *Archives of General Psychiatry*, 1960, 2, 434–440.

SULLIVAN, H. S.   *The interpersonal theory of psychiatry*. New York: Norton, 1953.

SZASZ, T. S.   *Pain and pleasure*. New York: Basic Books, 1957.

SZASZ, T. S.   *The myth of mental illness*. New York: Harper, 1961.

SZASZ, T. S.   *Law, liberty and psychiatry*. New York: Macmillan, 1963.

SZASZ, T. S.   *The ethics of psychoanalysis*. New York: Basic Books, 1965.

SZASZ, T. S.   Behavior therapy and psychoanalysis. *Medical Opinion and Review*, 1967, 3, 24–29.

THOMPSON, C. The role of the analyst's personality in therapy. *American Journal of Psychotherapy,* 1956 **10**, 347–359.

TRUAX, C. B., & CARKHUFF, R. R. Personality change in hospitalized mental patients during group psychotherapy as a function of the use of alternate sessions and vicarious therapy pretraining. *Journal of Clinical Psychology,* 1965, **21**, 225–228.

TRUAX, C. B., & CARKHUFF, R. R. *Toward effective counseling and psychotherapy: Training and practice.* Chicago: Aldine, 1967.

WASKOW, I. E. Counselor attitude and client behavior. *Journal of Consulting Psychology,* 1963, **27**, 405–412.

WATSON, J. B., & RAYNER, R. Conditioned emotional reactions. *Journal of Experimental Psychology,* 1920, **3**, 1–14.

WEITZMAN, B. Behavior therapy and psychotherapy. *Psychological Review,* 1967, **74**, 300–317.

WELKOWITZ, J., COHEN, J., & ORTMEYER, D. Value system similarity: Investigation of patient-therapist dyads. *Journal of Consulting Psychology,* 1967, **31**, 48–55.

WHITE, A. M., FICHTENBAUM, L., & DOLLARD, J. Evaluation of silence in initial interviews with psychiatric clinic patients. *Journal of Nervous and Mental Disease,* 1964, **139**, 550–557.

WHITEHORN, J. C., & BETZ, B. J. A study of psychotherapeutic relationships between physicians and schizophrenic patients. *American Journal of Psychiatry,* 1954, **111**, 321–331.

WHITEHORN, J. C. & BETZ, B. J. Further studies of the doctor as a crucial variable in the outcome of treatment with schizophrenic patients. *American Journal of Psychiatry,* 1960, **117**, 215–223.

WOLF, A. Group psychotherapy. In A. M. Freedman & H. I. Kaplan (Eds.), *Comprehensive textbook of psychiatry.* Baltimore: Williams & Wilkins, 1967. Pp. 1234–1241.

WOLPE, J. *Psychotherapy by reciprocal inhibition.* Stanford, Calif.: Stanford, 1958.

WOLPE, J. Reciprocal inhibition as the main basis of psychotherapeutic effects. In H. J. Eysenck (Ed.), *Behavior therapy and the neuroses.* New York: Pergamon, 1960. Pp. 88–113.

WOODGER, J. H. *Physics, psychology and medicine.* New York: Cambridge University Press, 1956.

GLOSSARY

Abreaction: Discharge of emotion resulting from the recall of a repressed idea or memory, often used synonymously with *catharsis.*

Analogue, experimental: An investigation in which the phenomena are simulated in a laboratory setting for the purpose of achieving greater experimental control.

Atomism: In psychology, the view that in order to understand personality and behavior, the phenomena must be broken down into smallest possible units. Antonym: *Holism.*

Autism, early infantile: A term coined by Kanner to refer to extreme withdrawal, self-absorption, and inability to form the usual interpersonal relationships in childhood.

Behaviorism: A term coined by J. B. Watson to indicate that all habits may be explained in terms of conditioned glandular and motor reaction. Consciousness, in particular, is rejected as a usable concept.

Catatonia: A syndrome, most frequently occurring with schizophrenia, characterized by muscular rigidity and mental stupor, sometimes alternating with excitement and confusion.

Catharsis: See *Abreaction.*

Client-centered therapy: A form of psychotherapy, developed by Carl R. Rogers, which places emphasis on the client's personal world and selfhood; diagnosis, evaluation, and deliberate behavior change by the therapist are eschewed.

Clinical psychology: That branch of psychology which focuses primarily upon the study, diagnosis, and treatment of psychological disorders.

Conditioning, operant: An approach to behavior modification, based on the views of B. F. Skinner, which stresses the control of behavior by manipulating its consequences.

Conditioning, respondent (classical):   Association of response with a previously unrelated stimulus through repeated presentation of the stimulus simultaneously with a stimulus normally yielding that response.

Conflict: The opposition of intrapsychic impulses. The core of a conflict is typically unconscious.

Content analysis: Any of a variety of procedures designed to quantify the meanings of human communications.

Control group: In scientific research, a standard against which the effects of an experimental manipulation are measured; specifically, a group of individuals which is comparable to the experimental group but which is not subjected to the procedure under investigation.

Conversion reaction: See *Hysteria.*

Countertransference: A term coined by Freud to designate the therapist's feelings and emotional reactions to the patient which tend to interfere with his objectivity and complicate the therapeutic interaction.

Defense (mechanism):   Any of a variety of unconscious reactions, usually involving repression, designed to protect the ego from the experience of anxiety or guilt associated with an unconscious wish or idea.

Desensitization: A psychotherapeutic procedure developed by J. Wolpe and designed to treat phobic reactions; its intent is to substitute a coping response antagonistic to anxiety. Self-assertion and relaxation are typical examples of such responses.

Dynamic: See *Psychodynamic.*

Eclectic: Selecting what appears to be best in various doctrines, methods, or styles; as for example, an eclectic orientation in psychotherapy.

Ego psychology: That trend in psychology which emphasizes the ego functions of the personality in theory, research, and clinical practice.

Electroconvulsive therapy: Shock therapy administered by means of electric currents; considered to be of therapeutic value in severe depressions and other major emotional disorders.

Empathy: An intellectual understanding of the thoughts and feelings of another person; a form of identification.

Enuresis: Bed-wetting by individuals who are capable of bladder control; often regarded as a neurotic symptom.

Existentialism: A philosophical and psychological movement emphasizing man's responsibility for leading the life he chooses to lead. Personal freedom, personal commitment, and personal decision are similarly stressed.

Holism: The view that man's personality cannot be broken down into elements, that man must be understood as a total person. Antonym: *Atomism.*

Hysteria: A psychoneurosis characterized by a physical symptom (e.g., paralysis) without structural lesion. The term *conversion hysteria* signifies that psychic energy has been "converted" into a physical symptom which expresses the conflict symbolically.

Insulin shock: A shock reaction produced by administration of insulin which lowers blood sugar; considered to be of therapeutic value in treating severe emotional disorders.

Kinesics: The study of body motion as related to speech.

Lay analyst: A person who has been trained in the psychoanalytic method of psychotherapy but who does not have a medical degree. (See also *Psychoanalyst, Psychotherapist.*)

Lobotomy: A form of psychosurgery consisting of severing nerve fibers in the frontal lobes of the cerebral cortex; considered to be of therapeutic value in treating severe emotional disorders.

Molar: In psychology, pertaining to the person as a whole, as contrasted with molecular. (See also *Holism.*)

Neurosis: See *Psychoneurosis.*

Nosology: The study of diseases and, particularly, of the classification of diseases or disorders.

Obsessive-compulsive neurosis: A neurosis characterized by intruding thoughts and by repetitive impulses to perform certain acts (e.g., hand-washing).

Phenomenology: The description of phenomena without attempt at interpretation or evaluation as, for example, in self-reports of feeling states.

Phobia: A neurotic anxiety reaction to a specific object or situation, as distinguished from generalized ("free-floating") anxiety.

Placebo: A substance having no pharmacological effect but accepted by the patient as having therapeutic value; *placebo reaction* refers to effects producted by pharmacological agents or psychological means regarded as having no therapeutic effects in themselves.

Prognosis: Forecast or estimation of the course, duration, and outcome of an illness or disorder.

Psychiatric social worker: A social worker with specialized training in the mental health field.

Psychiatrist: A physician who specializes in the treatment of mental illness.

Psychoanalyst: A person trained in the theory and practice of psychoanalysis. (See also *Psychotherapist; Psychiatrist; Lay analyst.*)

Psychodynamic: Refers to the forces of the mind. A phobia, for example, is viewed as representing the results of activity of psychic forces. *Psychodynamics* is the science of mental forces in action.

Psychoneurosis (also *Neurosis*):   A psychological disorder often characterized by (1) sensory, motor, or visceral disturbances, (2) anxiety, (3) troublesome thoughts, (4) sleep disturbances, (5) sexual disturbances, (6) general inhibition. Reality contact remains similar to that of the rest of the community.

Psychopath: See *Sociopath.*

Psychopathology: The study of mental disorders.

Psychosis: A serious mental disturbance, usually involving marked distortions of reality. Often but not always characterized by strange and bizarre feelings, beliefs, and behaviors. Roughly equivalent to the colloquial and legal term *insanity,* which, however, no longer has scientific standing. (See also *Schizophrenia.*)

Psychosomatic: Relating to organic malfunction or disease in which psychological factors play a part.

Psychotherapist: Generic term to describe a person trained in the theory and practice of psychotherapy. A psychoanalyst is a psychotherapist. (See also *Psychoanalyst; Psychiatrist.*)

Q-sort: A set of personality descriptions printed on individual cards, which the subject is asked to sort in terms of their applicability to him, etc. Provides clues concerning such constructs as self-concept.

Reciprocal inhibition: A concept formulated by J. Wolpe to the effect that anxiety responses can be abolished by training an individual to make an antagonistic response; a form of counterconditioning. (See also **Desensitization.**)

Reductionism: In psychology, an effort to explain complex phenomena by breaking them down into small components. (See also **Holism, Atomism.**)

Replication: Duplication of an experiment to test stability of previous results.

Resistance: In psychoanalysis and other forms of psychotherapy, the patient's unconscious opposition to treatment.

Rorschach Test: A projective psychological test, named after the Swiss psychiatrist Hermann Rorschach, consisting of a series of ink blots. A subject's responses provide clues to his personality, fantasy life, etc.

Schizophrenia: A group of psychoses often characterized by serious distortions of thinking and feeling, delusions, hallucinations, and bizarre behavior. (See also **Psychosis.**)

Sociopath, sociopathic (also *psychopath, psychopathic*):   A diagnostic term used to refer to a marked incapacity to restrain antisocial impulses accompanied by a normal awareness of the laws and mores and of the consequences of their violation. The psychopath tends to project the blame for his actions on others.

Thematic Apperception Test (TAT):   A projective psychological test developed by H. A. Murray consisting of a series of ambiguous scenes about which the subject is instructed to tell a story.

Transference: In psychoanalytic therapy, the projection of feelings, thoughts, and wishes onto the analyst, who has come to represent an object from the patient's past. The term *transference neurosis* refers to an intense form of the transference occurring typically in psychoanalytic treatment.

Unconditional positive regard: A concept in client-centered therapy which refers to the requirement that the therapist must accept the client as a person, without qualification.

Vicarious learning: Acquisition of a skill by observing others learning it.

Working through: The sustained effort required in psychotherapy to overcome conscious and unconscious resistances, thereby resolving or ameliorating neurotic patterns.

Name Index

Name Index

Imber, S. D., 123, 126, 180, 182, 184
Isaacs, K. S., 124, 180

Jackson, D., 72
Jacobson, E., 57
Jones, E., 96, 180
Jones, M. C., 75, 180
Jung, C. G., 31

Kanner, L., 187
Kaplan, F., 127, 180
Keith-Spiegel, P., 125, 180
Kessel, L., 96, 180
Kiesler, D. J., 38, 107, 135, 183
Klein, M., 31
Knight, R. P., 96, 181
Krasner, L., 64, 115, 133, 135, 181
Kubie, L. S., 173, 175, 181
Kuhn, T. H., 152

Lang, P. J., 75, 181
Lazarus, A. A., 64
Lennard, H. L., 124, 181
Lessler, K., 126, 185
Levitt, E. E., 124, 175, 181
Lieberman, M. A., 81
Lippitt, G. L., 71, 177
Lipsher, D., 117, 177
Lohrenz, J. G., 125, 181
Lorr, M., 116, 118, 182
Lovaas, O. I., 59, 181
Lubin, B., 175
Luborsky, L., 84, 97, 108, 115, 126, 135, 173, 176, 180, 181, 185

McGaugh, J. L., 60, 62–64, 177
McNair, D. M., 116, 118, 182
Mann, J., 71, 80, 182
Marks, I. M., 122, 126, 179
Marmor, J., 35

Marsden, G., 131, 135, 181
Massimo, J. L., 127, 181
Matarazzo, J. D., 84, 107, 133, 135, 182, 184
May, R., 143, 145, 152, 182
Mead, G. H., 39
Melamed, B. G., 181
Menninger, K., 35
Miles, M. B., 71, 182
Miller, P., 117, 177
Mohr, J. P., 58, 176
Moreno, J. L., 67
Mosak, H. H., 45, 46, 184
Munroe, R. L., 35
Murray, E. J., 131, 176
Murray, H. A., 191
Myers, J. K., 125, 176

Nash, E. H., 123, 126, 180, 182, 184
Newman, R. G., 21, 78, 183

Oppenheimer, J. R., 152
Orlinsky, D. E., 132, 182
Ortmeyer, D., 116, 186
Otto, H. A., 71, 80, 182
Overall, B., 124, 182

Parloff, M. B., 84, 107, 183
Paul, G., 100, 103–106, 122, 182
Pavlov, I. P., 54–56, 107
Pearl, A., 157, 183
Pittenger, R. E., 132, 182
Polanyi, M., 152
Pope, A., 144
Poser, E., 125, 182

Rank, O., 31, 39, 73
Raush, H. L., 115, 182
Rayner, R., 75, 186

Redlich, F. C., 21, 78, 125, 180
Reich, W., 31
Reik, T., 21
Reisel, J., 80
Rice, L. N., 117, 131, 183
Riessman, F., 157, 183
Rioch, D., 93
Rioch, M. J., 78, 175, 183
Rogers, C. R., 38, 39, 41, 43, 44, 47, 49, 50, 73, 107, 115, 123, 131, 135, 139, 142, 145, 153, 183, 187
Rorschach, H., 191
Rosenthal, D., 116, 163, 183
Rosenzweig, S., 97, 183
Rubinstein, E. A., 84, 107, 183
Russell, B., 144, 184

Sandifer, M. G., 87, 184
Sargent, H. D., 135
Sartre, J. P., 39
Saslow, G., 133, 135, 182
Satir, V., 72, 80
Savage, C., 84, 107, 184
Schaeffer, B., 181
Schein, E. H., 69, 80, 184
Schofield, W., 174, 175, 184
Schutz, W. C., 80
Schwartz, E. K., 81
Schwartzman, A. E., 125, 181
Sechrest, L. B., 107, 127, 128, 179
Shlien, J. M., 45, 46, 84, 107, 184
Shore, M. F., 127, 181
Shumaker, E., 127, 177
Sifneos, P. E., 127, 184
Silber, E., 78, 183
Silverman, J., 124, 127, 179
Simmons, J. Q., 181
Skinner, B. F., 54–56, 58, 61, 153, 188
Slack, C. W., 78, 184
Slavson, S. R., 68, 80
Solomon, L. N., 71, 177
Spiegel, D., 125, 180

Stanley, J., 135
Stephens, J. H., 126, 184
Stoler, N., 116, 184
Stoller, F. H., 71, 184
Stone, A. R., 123, 126, 180, 182, 184
Straus, E., 145
Strupp, H. H., 84, 97, 108, 110, 117, 121, 123, 125, 126, 132, 135, 142, 149, 163, 184, 185
Sullivan, H. S., 8, 21, 32, 35, 39, 185
Szasz, T. S., 7, 21, 120, 144, 153, 156, 159, 160, 165, 185

Thompson, C., 32, 111, 186
Thorndike, E. L., 54
Timbury, G. C., 87, 184
Trosman, H., 124, 180
Truax, C. B., 38, 108, 115, 123, 125, 126, 132, 135, 175, 177, 186

Ullmann, L. P., 64
Urban, H. B., 21, 134, 152, 178
Usdansky, B. S., 78, 183

Vogel, J. L., 117, 178

Wagstaff, A. K., 183
Wallach, M. S., 185
Wann, T. W., 153
Waskow, I. E., 116, 186
Watson, J. B., 53, 75, 186, 187
Weitzman, B., 63, 186
Welkowitz, J., 116, 186
Weschler, I. R., 80
Whitaker, D. S., 81
White, A. M., 123, 186

Whitehorn, J. C., 117, 119, 186
Wiens, A. N., 133, 135, 182
Williams, J. V., 117, 123, 125, 185
Wolberg, L. R., 21
Wolf, A., 67, 81, 186
Wolff, H. H., 122, 126, 179
Wolman, B. B., 175

Wolpe, J., 55–58, 60, 62–64, 102, 186, 188, 191
Woodger, J. H., 146, 186

Yamamoto, J., 124, 127, 179

Zilboorg, G., 35

Subject Index

Subject Index

Psychologist, clinical training for, 171

(*See also* Psychotherapist)

Psychoneurosis:

definition of, 190

disease model: inadequacy of, 6–7, 120

unacceptability of, for behaviorists, 52–53

as problem in living, 5–7

theory of: behavior therapy, 54

psychoanalytic, 26

treatment for, 97

through psychoanalysis, 97, 121

(*See also* Psychotherapy; Spontaneous improvement)

(*See also* Hysteria; Obsessive-compulsive; Phobia)

Psychopath:

definition of, 121, 190, 191

treatment for, unsuitability of psychoanalysis, 121

(*See also* Sociopath)

Psychopathology, definition of, 12, 112, 190

Psychosis:

definition of, 190

theory of, in behavior therapy, 54

treatment of: behavior therapy, 55

psychoanalysis, 121

(*See also* Autism; Schizophrenia)

Psychosomatic disease, definition of, 190

Psychosomatic medicine, 6

Psychotherapist:

definition of, 3, 8, 190

didactic or training analysis for, 114, 170

in-therapy behavior, studies of, 131–133

nonprofessional as, 59, 78–79, 174–175

-patient matching, 111

-patient relationship, 12–15, 123–125

Psychotherapist:

as a research variable, 110, 111, 113–120

experience level, 117, 132

interest and liking, 116–117

personality, 93–94, 112, 114–116

theoretical orientation, 117

values, 116

warmth, acceptance, and empathy, 115–116

role and function of, 7–14, 16–17

in client-centered psychotherapy, 40–43

contrasted with physician, 2–5, 8

as human communication specialist, 11

in psychoanalytic psychotherapy, 28–29

as researcher-scientist, 16–17

training of, 168–175

existing, 168–172

proposed, 172–175

"type" (A & B), 117–119

(*See also* Lay analyst; Psychiatric social worker; Psychiatrist; Psychoanalyst; Psychologist; Psychotherapy)

Psychotherapy:

as a contractual agreement, 156–157

definition of, 2, 15

problems in defining, 92–94

effectiveness of, 17–19, 110

criteria for, 18, 88–89

Eysenck's research, 52, 94–100

emotional experience in, 12, 27–28

ethics, 156–165

experiential learning in, 12, 143–145

goals, 9–11, 15, 105

as a human relationship, 4, 14

length, 14

medical model, 157–158

Rorschach Test, definition of, 139, 191

Schizophrenia:
 biochemical-psychological inter-play, 9n.
 definition of, 191
 treatment, unsuitability of psychoanalysis, 121
 (See also Psychosis)
Sociopath, definition of, 191
 (See also Psychopath)
Spontaneous improvement, 90–91, 97–99
Symptoms:
 behavior therapy: classical view of, 55, 62–63
  focus on, 53, 87–89, 105
  operant view of, 56, 62–63
 client-centered therapy, view of, 42
 dynamic-oriented therapy, de-emphasis of, 87, 89, 105
 generalization of relief, 105–106
 leading to psychotherapy, 2–3, 5–6, 9–11
 multiple nature of, 87, 89
 psychoanalytic therapy, view of, 25, 62–63
 psychogenic, 3
 -substitution, 63, 103

Thematic Apperception Test (TAT), definition of, 124, 191
Theoretical viewpoints (systems), 14–16
 (See also Behavior therapy; Client-centered psychotherapy; Psychoanalytic psychotherapy; Psychotherapy)
Therapist (see Psychotherapist)
Tranquilizer, 3, 5
Transference:
 definition of, 25, 27, 191
 therapeutic value, 27–28
Transference neurosis:
 created by psychoanalytic therapy, 93
  definition of, 191
 as form of psychoneurosis, 34, 121

Unconditional positive regard:
 definition of, 191
 of therapist, 41–42

Vicarious learning, 133
 definition of, 192

Working through, definition of, 29, 192